GAME FREE

GAME FREE

A Guide to the
Meaning of Intimacy

Thomas C. Oden

HARPER & ROW, PUBLISHERS
New York, Evanston, San Francisco, London

FIRST EDITION

Library of Congress Cataloging in Publication Data

Oden, Thomas C
  Game free.
  Includes bibliographical references.
   1. Intimacy (Psychology) 2. Transactional analysis.
I. Title.
BF575.I5O33   158.2   73–18687
ISBN 0–06–066343–X

FOR EDRITA

with whom I have experienced the game-free relationship

CONTENTS

Preface

Three themes have attracted my attention in the discussion that follows: intimacy, transactional analysis, and the religious dimensions of the interpersonal life.

My subject matter may best be clarified by viewing it as a diagram of three concentric circles:

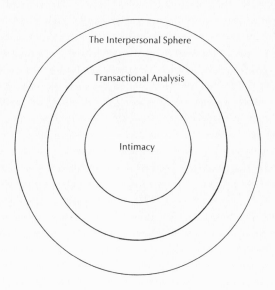

Accordingly, the inner circle or target of my interest is the question of intimacy: its definition, dynamics, dilemmas, ironies, and cultural implications (Part I).

Surrounding and including this target area, however, is another subject of keen interest to many today, the transactional analysis of Eric Berne and his followers, which offers not only a way of understanding intimacy but more generally an approach to the analysis of all interpersonal transactions. Part II of this study develops an interpretation and critique of transactional analysis that both appreciates the achievements of TA and yet hopes to move beyond some of the territory it has already explored. So regardless of whether the reader is inclined either negatively or positively toward transactional analysis, he or she is invited to follow the path of this argument in search of a way of grasping the inner core of transactional analysis and moving beyond it.

The larger sphere of my interest, which includes the other two, is more generally the interpersonal life, with special reference to its religious dimension (Part III). When persons meet they find themselves in touch with that which transcends their interpersonal meeting. It is this widely experienced awareness that deserves not only our best psychological and empirical analysis but also our richest resources of philosophical and theological wisdom.

In seeking to do relative justice to this intriguing subject matter, I have benefited enormously not only from the wide-ranging literature that the footnotes indicate, but more so from exceptional insights gained through give-and-take dialogue with friends, colleagues, students, and groups with whom I have worked. Among those to whom I owe special thanks, either for critically reading the manuscript or for perceptively grappling with its issues, are Will Herberg, Pieter de Jong, Lawrence D. McIntosh, Shirley Sugerman Rosenberg, Fred W. Paddock, Ann Boyd, Judith Kupfer Nordin, W. Jene Miller, Robert Ball, Young Ho Chun, Philip G. Hanson, Larry Mart, and Thomas A. Harris, and above all the challenging students in my classes on interpersonal theology at Phillips Seminary, The Institute of Religion, in Houston and at Drew University, the Theological and Graduate Schools. Finally, for providing me with a sustained relation of enriching intimacy not only during the time this book was being conceived and written, but for over twenty years now, I am inexpressibly grateful to my own covenant partner, Edrita.

T.C.O.

Drew Forest
Madison, New Jersey

I. INTERPERSONAL COMMUNION

My purposes in Part I are: (1) to construct a working definition of intimacy by clarifying the basic ironies of the intimate relationship, probing the history of the language of intimacy, and by descriptively reporting accounts of how persons felt in moments of intimate experiencing; (2) to try to understand why intimacy is both anxiously desired in our society and yet often fiercely resisted by those who seem most to desire it, and why sexuality that seeks intimacy can ironically become an obstacle to intimacy; and (3) to present evidence for the hypothesis that effective psychotherapy is a surrogate intimacy.

1

1. Intimacy: A Definition

In searching for a working definition of intimacy, the first tasks are: (1) to track some of the intriguing images of the language of intimacy; (2) to present a collage of impressionistic descriptions of how persons have felt in moments of intense personal closeness; and (3) to thread our way through some of the potential contradictions and internal tensions present in the concept of intimacy.

The *Intimus* Sphere

I will be arguing that there is a relationship in which persons are in fact closer to each other than in genital sexuality. It can occur with or without sexuality. It is a relationship in which two persons, even at great physical distance, may be deeply responsive to the inner reality of each other. It is called intimacy.

Much sexuality, to be sure, has the quality of intimacy. But genital orgasm can and often does occur without intimacy, and even as an offense against it.

While intimacy can emerge within the framework of sexuality, intimacy is never adequately defined by sexuality. To view intimacy only as an aspect of sexuality is a peculiar misjudgment of popular modern consciousness.

Not everyone, of course, is desperately looking for intimacy. Although for some this search takes an urgent and overt form, for most it takes a quiet form of waiting and yearning to receive. Yet it remains a basic question for most persons in our society: How can I come close to others without risking something essential to myself?

What do we want when we want intimacy? Intimacy, according to its dictionary definition, is the quality or condition of being close to another, a warmly personal being-together characterized by self-disclosure and affection. It is the experience of close, sustained familiarity with another's inner life.[1]

Intimacy has long been a euphemism for sexual closeness, but it can also refer to the closeness of friends, family, neighbors, close associates. It deepens when sustained over a duration of time. Insofar as one experiences an intimate relation he experiences a beholding of another person in his or her essential depth; he knows the other person from the inside out, deeply, internally.

The Latin word for inner or innermost is *intimus*. If one knows, grasps, the internal reality of someone he grasps the *intimus*, the inmost character of the person.[2] Similarly, in many other languages the root word for intimacy refers to this "most internal" quality. The German word for intimacy, *Innigkeit*, especially conveys this quality of inwardness or internal awareness. If something is *innig* it is inward, heartfelt, sincere, responsive, deep—in short, intimate. To the degree that one experiences the *intimum* of another, or feels another's *Innigkeit*, he is aware of the internal sphere, the most inward reality of the other.

Influenced by this nuance of innermost, our English word *intimate* points to a particular kind of knowing, a knowledge of the core of something, an understanding of the inmost parts, that which is indicative of one's deepest nature and marked by close physical, mental, or social association. The biblical word for sexual closeness is this sort of knowing: "Adam knew Eve." When I am in touch with the *intimum* of another, I know that which is ordinarily hidden from public view yet revealed in the closeness and vulnerability of the relationship. When I am aware that someone else is in touch with my own *intimum* I know

I have been reached at the deeper levels of my consciousness. One does not often reveal or open up one's *intimum* to another. It does not occur easily or readily, even though a certain outward appearance of intimacy may be easy for some to project.[3]

The English word *intimacy* has also taken on the nuance of being a complete intermixture, a compounding or interweaving of things.[4] The closeness is such that "it would call for some effort to disentangle a relationship of things marked by such intimacy."[5]

Although we may speak of intimacy in connection with objects, it more properly refers to persons. One is not intimate *with* things, but may have an intimate knowledge *of* things. In this case the focus is on the closeness and depth of empathic understanding and experiencing of something. One may have an intimate knowledge of an automobile, a garden, a space guidance system, or an eighteenth-century town, and in each case we are speaking of close, detailed inward knowledge of that thing. We are pointing to a sustained experiential knowledge of something in which one has participated and knows "from the inside."

Since the essence of an intimate personal relation is shared experience of each other's interior life, any description that might tend to perceive intimacy as an event in *individual* consciousness would be defective. Whatever it is we mean when we speak of personal intimacy, at least it is something that occurs only in the emotive flow and resonance *between* two persons. The locus is precisely the *relation*,[6] not individual consciousness, although one may experience its flow in individual consciousness.

Thus it is not possible to be intimate with one who does not want to be intimate. Intimacy exists only by mutual consent, never by unilateral desire. If one person wants closeness with another who does not want closeness, then the relation is not intimate. It may be described as a unilateral affection, but not intimacy, where the emotive flow moves both ways.

Furthermore, it is a misunderstanding of intimacy to conceive of it purely as an active relationship of knowing. For there is also the receptive side of one's experiencing oneself as being known by another. It is in the twofold flow of caring and being cared about, of loving and being loved, of knowing and being known, that intimacy occurs.[7]

The study of marital intimacy by Howard and Charlotte Clinebell[8] usefully distinguished twelve different types or strata of intimacy that apply to many close relationships. These twelve types can serve as a beginning point for our exploration of the wide range of intimate relationships. Intimacy is not just one thing, but many, and these twelve strata, however briefly described, show its multiform character:

Sexual intimacy (erotic or orgasmic closeness)
Emotional intimacy (being tuned to each other's wavelength)
Intellectual intimacy (closeness in the world of ideas)
Aesthetic intimacy (sharing experiences of beauty)
Creative intimacy (Sharing in acts of creating together)
Recreational intimacy (relating in experiences of fun and play)
Work intimacy (the closeness of sharing common tasks)
Crisis intimacy (closeness in coping with problems and pain)
Conflict intimacy (facing and struggling with differences)
Commitment intimacy (mutuality derived from common self-investment)
Spiritual intimacy (the we-ness in sharing ultimate concerns)
Communication intimacy (the source of all types of true intimacy)

These twelve strata of intimacy have been used by the Clinebells as the basis of an action-meditation for marital intimates. I present them early in our discussion without comment as a potential meditation on the varieties of intimacy and as a transition into our next section, which will explore some of these varieties.

The Intimate Experience: A Collage of Descriptions

The nature and dynamics of intimacy have received only scant attention by researchers. Not much data has been accumulated by the behavioral sciences on the phenomenon of intimacy. Although many writers (Bach, Berne, Schutz, Lowen, Goodman, Mazur)[9] make frequent use of the concept, few have attempted to define clearly what they mean by it. To my knowledge there is no definitive study of intimacy available in any language.

In order to begin to build a body of descriptive data on the nature and dynamics of intimacy, I have asked groups of persons with whom I have been working to recall in fantasy a moment of intense closeness or warm personal fulfillment with another person, to behold in imagination a specific time of genuine, fulfilling intimacy, to remember the colors, shapes, sounds, and feelings of that relationship, to stay with the fantasy long enough to savor it, so as to be there with the other in memory and imagination. Then I have asked them to write down in clear, descriptive language what it is they have experienced.[10]

I have collected and studied a considerable number of these remembered experiences of intimacy, resulting in a remarkable correlation of factors that recur when people describe intimate experiencing. From these experiential accounts it has become clear that there are many different forms, settings, and qualities of intimacy, yet some characteristic features pervade the descriptions repeatedly. What follows is an attempt to summarize some of these correlations.

Although such varied experiencing is difficult to reduce to categories,[11] the descriptions seem to fall generally into two distinguishable, though inseparable, levels of awareness: the interpersonal and the transpersonal. By interpersonal I mean that which is happening between the persons. By transpersonal I refer to that which transcends the persons, the awareness of awe, mystery, and gift, the sense that the relationship reflects the inner meaning of history that transcends the particular persons.[12]

Rather than belaboring a statistical correlation of the variables of these data, I would prefer to deal with them in a more impressionistic fashion. Using Abraham Maslow's method[13] in reporting peak experiences, I will present the correlated accounts in the form of a collage or impressionistic portraiture of recurrent ways in which persons experience close relationships.

INTERPERSONAL AWARENESS

How do intimates describe moments of fulfillment? Here is a sampling.

Spontaneity, feeling-flow, openness. Many intimates remember feeling exceptionally in touch with their own here-and-now experiencing in moments of personal intimacy. They are relaxed, spontaneous, and willing to trust their own feelings. They are not internally blocked.

Many speak of an extraordinarily high degree of self-awareness and lucidity in the experience of intimacy. They speak of self-acceptance, inner harmony, feeling "the freedom to be me," feeling confident in the unfolding of their experiencing process, trusting that unfolding; feeling integrated, understanding oneself, discovering insights about oneself. All of these hinge on the experience of heightened self-awareness in the context of an intimate relationship.

Some felt able to unload their feelings toward each other, even if negative. They felt able to get things off their chest. They experienced a relationship of uncommon trust, where the other person was perceived as radically trustworthy.

Some reported a previously undiscovered capacity for honesty and deep leveling with the other, even if it meant facing anger or rejection. They found themselves able to risk conflict and work through it together. They were nondefensive and unashamed. Some described the experience as one of emotive nakedness with no defenses between them.[14]

Closeness, presence, availability. Common to most descriptions is an intense closeness with the other. Some described this as a kind of at-oneness or communion with the other person, even in some cases to the extent of feeling that they are as a single organism, so that the two become "one flesh."[15]

The intimate experience is described by some as one of sheer joy in the mere presence of the other; as being for the other, being in touch with the other's feelings, being aware of the profound goodness of the other; being willing to let the other be himself and experiencing the permission of the other to be oneself.

Some speak of the decisive importance to them of simple presence to another. For them the simple beholding of the partner is the most memorable aspect of the intimate moment. The mere being with another, the feeling that one is fully with the other, is the fundament of the experience of intimacy.[16]

Some speak of the radical availability of the partner. The partner is fully there with no blockages—open, warm, attentive, accepting. The attention and care flows both ways.

More frequently the intimate relationship is described quite simply as one of being loved and loving. It is the awareness that one is cared for, appreciated, desired, and that the care, appreciation, and desire are mutual, even in spite of imperfection and inadequacies.

Sharing, renewing, beholding. Others remember their intimate experiencing as one of sacrificing together amid arduous tasks. They knew the sense of belonging that comes from shared experiencing. Some described a moment of recommitment to an important task as a moment of intense intimacy, wherein both persons were mutually grasped by the excitement or gravity of a commitment to a long-range fate-laden decision. They felt very close to their partner at the moment when the commitment was decided or redecided.

Some experienced a special intimacy in being with an intimate in the context of having lost another intimate through alienation or death. The depth of one relationship illuminated and bestowed meaning on the other. Repeatedly persons reported exceptional lucidity in the presence of the death of an intimate, where the meaning of a person's life, previously undisclosed, seemed to become clear. Intimates often felt needed, wanted, or accepted, particularly in situations where urgent or desperate need was evident.

Some describe the intimate experience in aesthetic terms, as a mutual beholding of unspeakable beauty. Others experience intimacy as a time of shared creativity, of the release of constructive energies, or as the mutual shaping of something together.

Ecstacy, freedom, levity. Intensely intimate experiencing is sometimes described as an ecstacy, an overflow of feelings, beyond words. One cannot contain the joy; it is too much to express; one feels inexpressibly happy, soaring, elated, high, tingles, chills, exhilarated, expansive. "I wanted to dance, shout and yell forever," one wrote.

Many viewed intimate experiencing under an orgasmic analogy: the ecstatic explosion of feelings of love in full bodily and spiritual presence and unity with the other.

Others did not experience a highly ecstatic intimacy, but instead reported a varied range of close experiencing over a longer period of time, where closeness at various strata illuminated or radiated into closeness at other strata.

Intimacy is often described in relation to *freedom,* both as a moment in which one feels freedom *for* the other and freedom *from* anxiety, guilt, or boredom in the presence of another.

Similarly some describe intimate experiencing as a sense of release, as if a weight were lifted, the weight of loneliness; or as a victory, as if one had come currently to experience precisely that for which one had hoped, sometimes accompanied by a sense of lightness, giddiness, or levity.

TRANSPERSONAL AWARENESS

Awe, cohesion, letting-be. A surprising number of descriptions speak of intimate experiencing in the language of awe, such as the awe one experiences at the presence of birth or death, or in the presence of the struggle of another person through crisis.

In the intimate experience some became aware of the intrinsic value of life, the intense prizing of simple being, the sense that life is profoundly meaningful beyond its seeming incongruities. Some experienced life as a unity, as if in that moment all things seemed "put together." They celebrated their aliveness. They found themselves surprised to discover that "I am really here with you and really alive."

Giftlike quality, surprise. Many experience intimacy as a profound gift. There is an unearned, undeserved dimension, an aura of sheer grace in the relationship. Persons experience the presence of another in a very close relationship as something they cannot control or manipulate but a presence that comes to them, a relation that is bestowed. They may have to struggle for it, and work to achieve the conditions in which intimacy might occur, but it is not controlled or determined by these conditions. One must wait for it to occur, and when it does it is experienced as a profound gift.

Consequently many felt a profound sense of gratitude. They felt deeply privileged to be there. Others felt deeply humbled in the presence of that gift, and sensed the fragility and finitude of human relationships this side of death.[17]

One woman wrote, "Suddenly we looked at each other and asked how long it had been that we were together. Surprisingly fifteen years. We laughed and said, 'Well, I guess the trial period is over!' It was a wonderful warm feeling. Her friends had become mine—mine had become hers. Many things we had enjoyed together—concerts, theater, friends, and families; but we were not dependent on doing things always together. We experienced an enlargement of interest and a deepening of the joys of life in each other's presence—also a sharing of difficulties and sorrows. Sounds like a Pollyanna story, doesn't it? But the enjoyment and mutual appreciativeness was really just that. Mutual trust, I believe, was at the core of the relationship, broken by her death, but still alive."

Mystery, timelessness, wholeness. Many descriptions pointed to the mystery in interpersonal communion, the sense of wonder in the presence of an immensely valued human being who is capable of love, amazed that "it could happen to me." A significant number spoke of intimacy as a moment of eternal awareness, or one in which the eternal now is present, where time loses its movement and one is wholly there with the inner meaning of the cosmos in and through the here-and-now relationship.[18]

Finally, many experienced a sense of purposefulness in history that became intuitively clear through the relation with the partner. Whereas prior to the intimate moment things may have felt dislocated, fragmented, disordered, and broken up, in the moment of intimacy things seemed to cohere in a meaningful gestalt beyond all the tragedies of human existence.[19] This is expressed by some as a sense of wholeness or completion. It is a perspective on history that is focused and integrated through a relationship with another person, in which one feels a cosmic embrace through the embrace of the other.

This variety of intimate experiences may help us grasp something of the scope of intimacy. The purpose is not to pinpoint a definition of intimacy, but to paint an impressionistic portrait or put together a mosaic of moments of personal closeness. From here we proceed to explore some of the seeming paradoxes of the intimate relationship, in search of its basic definition.

The Intimate Relationship: Six Ironies

The six potential contradictions of the intimate relationship may be stated in terms of six questions.

1. What is the relation of intimacy to time? Is it sustained through time, or is it a moment of ecstatic closeness that transcends time?

2. Is the covenant relationship fixed and without terminus, or is it continually renegotiated?

3. If the relationship is to a high degree empathic and self-giving, does not one risk the loss of self-identity and individuation?

4. If the relation is essentially warm and affirming, how does it deal with legitimate conflicts of interest? Must intimacy necessarily be forced into conflict-avoidance?

5. Can we assume truthfulness as an absolute norm of the intimate relationship without coercively requiring compulsive self-disclosure?

6. Is intimacy subject to or does it transcend death?

Each of the six answers will begin with a thesis statement (italicized) that will focus on essential points in tension and internal stresses that are at work in relationships of intimacy.

In two columns we can visualize the twelve basic dialectical points that grapple with the six questions and thus feed into a full definition of intimacy as follows:

Duration	Ecstacy
Accountability	Negotiability
Empathy	Congruence
Emotive Warmth	Conflict-capability
Self-disclosure	Letting-be
Finitude	Transcendence

No one of these twelve elements of the definition should be considered as artificially separable parts of the total gestalt of intimacy, but rather as dimensions of intimacy that exist in creative tension. Even though they do not all invariably occur with the same force in every intimate moment, they will in time emerge over the course of a sustained intimate relationship.

DURATION AND ECSTASY

An intimate relationship is ordinarily sustained over a period of time with a shared interpersonal memory, yet it may intensify in ecstatic moments of experiencing that render the other times relatively less vivid. The ecstatic moments, nonetheless, depend on the sustained history of personal covenant for their meaning. Thus there is a dialectical relation between duration and ecstasy.

The crucial distinction here is that between the sustained intimate relationship and the ecstatic intimate moment. Some confuse the two, assuming that when one experiences a brief moment of intense closeness with another, there exists consequently an intimate relationship. Our common language, however, understands the intimate relationship as one that endures, persists, and survives over a period of time. It must have a history. To the degree that it is not sustained in time, it has less chance of developing the profound sort of internal knowledge that we assume in our ordinary language about intimacy.

There is no instant intimacy,[20] even though the encounter culture appears to be trying to facilitate it on a brief basis. It succeeds to some extent, but the short-term relationships often yearn for sustenance in time, and thus for the conditions of true intimacy.

A sustained intimate relationship may suffer long periods of drought without an ecstatic moment. Yet when that moment occurs, it seems to feed the roots of the relationship and bring it new life, like a shower on tenacious plants in arid soil.

An essential dimension of deepening intimacy is shared memory. Persons who have been through conflict together and have understood each other's struggle often grow to be more profoundly intimate, since they are able to be more deeply aware of the *intimum* of the partner. The dispossessed, who have shared a common experience of suffering and subjugation, may have a greater capacity for certain kinds of intimacy with each other than with those who have not shared such experiences. Persons of wide differences, however, can through exceptional empathy develop intimate relationships.

There is a sense among intimates that they share something that is unique to them and them alone. This is why excessively generalized descriptions of intimacy remain unconvincing. Only those who have shared those particular ecstasies or struggles have the innermost knowledge of each other that intimacy apparently requires.

A Hebraic way of stating this is that all covenant relationships have a history. The people of Israel have a history. A marriage has a history. A friendship has a history. Each segment of that developing story is important to the illumination of the meaning of the relationship. In the history of Israel each period of the story illuminates the meaning of the original covenant in a fresh way. So also in the history of the Church, each historical period in which its proclamation is stated is the occasion for bestowing fresh significance on the originative event. Similarly, in the history of the covenant between two people, each crucial moment of struggle or crisis or alienation or ecstasy bestows a significance on the relationship that is stored in the memory of those who experience it. This means that covenant existence is historical existence. Relationships move through time; they are not simply suspended ahistorically in eternal moments. They each have their own story. This suggests that the Hebraic tradition, which is so particularly concerned with *the history of covenants*,[21] may be a more profound religious resource for understanding interpersonal covenants than are idealistic philosophies or eastern attempts to be detached from historical reality.

The term ecstasy may be too intense to describe the levels of feeling that many experience in intimate relationships. Friendships do not demand overflowing feelings of ecstasy in order to be deep and intimate. They may have moments of intensification, of beholding, of deep belly laughter, of moving affection, but that does not imply that the value of the relation is judged exclusively by its occasional ecstasy.

ACCOUNTABILITY AND NEGOTIABILITY

Is the covenant relationship fixed and without terminus, or is it continually renegotiated?

The ironic hypothesis that follows is that *intimate relationships are characterized by contractual clarity and enduring commitment on the assumption that mutual accountability is without a fixed terminus, and yet within that frame of reference they are forever being refashioned and renegotiated in their specific forms.*

Most contracts have a specific terminus. In a contract to deliver goods, for example, the moment the goods are delivered the contract is fulfilled. Intimate covenants are never "concluded" in that sense. The intimate relationship would be offended by the thought that it should have a designated end. Even though intimates are often separated by time and distance, still they resume the postures of closeness when they return, as if time and space could not overcome their covenant memory and hope.

The intimate relation is sustained in time as an act of covenant fidelity. It is a relation to which one commits oneself, as the service of matrimony says, "for better or for worse . . . in sickness and in health . . . till death us do part."[22] Thus when intimates confront obstacles such as dislocation, suffering, and frustration, these are not necessarily regarded as a threat to intimacy, but rather a healthy intimacy is seen as supportive of the attempt to deal constructively with these limitations.

While specific expectations are constantly being readjusted, intimates find themselves committed to each other in such a way that the presumption is on the side of the hope of continuance, so that whatever problems or obstacles arise, the assumption is that they will be worked out with mutual trust and accountability. This is one reason why the disruption or termination of relationships that were assumed to be intimate is shocking and painful both to intimates and third-party observers.

Yet, however bound together covenant partners may feel themselves to be, their continuing relationship requires that specific understandings be continuously open to restatement and sharpening. When the objective situation changes, or when consciousness changes, the expectations of partners change. Thus contract clarification is perennial expression of covenant bonding. Such renegotiations take place, however, within the larger frame of reference of enduring covenant fidelity.

To the degree that both persons find themselves accountable to clear and just covenants, the possibility of intimacy is intensified. The relation functions best when each intimate knows fairly accurately what the other wants and expects from the relationship, and when both are willing to call each other accountable to whatever covenants they have made.[23]

EMPATHY AND CONGRUENCE

If the relationship is to a high degree empathic, self-giving, and symbiotic, does not one risk the loss of self-identity and individuation?

In an intimate relationship, partners are singularly able to share each other's consciousness without loss of self-identity, since it is precisely amid the increased flow of empathy that one's individual self-awareness and identity is facilitated and intensified. In sum, intimacy enhances individual identity in the midst of deepening interpersonal encounter.

The same point can be stated differently: Through empathy, intimacy grows into a symbiosis (literally a "living together") of interdependent functions, and yet it is most intimate precisely at the point at which it enables partners to become more individuated, more fully their own unique selves.[24]

Still another attempt to state the same dialectic: Precisely to the degree that one is in touch with his feelings, to that degree he is able to facilitate his partner's empathy toward him. This point can be illuminated by exploring the relation between two crucial components of intimacy: empathy and congruence.[25] I am sufficiently convinced of the importance of empathy and congruence in the formation of intimacy that I will argue strongly that without certain levels of each the intimate relationship has little chance of surviving.

Since this may be *the* most crucial of the six dialectical issues, I will clarify it step by step, delineating first the way in which empathy enables intimacy, and second, the way in which congruence facilitates empathy.

Empathy is the process of placing oneself in the frame of reference of another, feeling the world as he feels it, sharing his world with him.[26] Insofar as intimates are able to feel their way accurately into the affect levels of their partner, intimacy is enhanced. The most descriptive colloquial phrase that expresses this notion is to "stand in his shoes," which means to project oneself imaginatively into how it feels to be him, standing there in his place, his situation.

The following schema, symbolizing two persons in interaction, will clarify the dynamics of empathy.

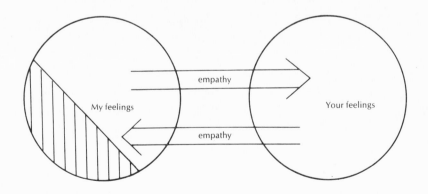

Empathy is capacity for one person to enter imaginatively into the sphere of consciousness of another, to feel the specific contours of another's experience, to allow one's imagination to risk entering the inner experiencing process *(intimus)* of another.

Some people have a readily recognizable capacity for empathy. When you meet such a person you know intuitively: This person understands. Others listen only to a very small part of you. They do not hear you at the feeling level and are less intimate-capable. For intimacy is relatively more possible to the degree that empathy is possible. A mutual flow of empathic understanding moves between the partners. Conversely, the promise of intimacy is relatively reduced to the degree that partners are not capable of accurately intuiting each other's feelings.

To the degree that I am able to experience myself as understood by my partner, and my partner experiences himself as understood by me, intimacy is possible. This is very near the essential definition of intimacy, since in a mutual flow of empathic understanding we are both giving each other the opportunity to see what is inside us, what is most inward *(intimus)*. [27]

Let us suppose, however, that there is a part of me that I would prefer *not* to be known by my partner. I put up blocks and resistances to prevent him or her from grasping and understanding that part of me. That would obviously reduce the level and promise of intimacy. There is a part of my inner reality *(intimum)* that I prevent the other from seeing, and in fact I must search for strategies and security operations to prevent my partner from knowing that part of me.

(Theological aside: In *Kerygma and Counseling*[28] I have argued that a remarkable analogy exists between the themes of human empathy and God's incarnation; for incarnation means that God assumes our frame of reference, entering fully into our human situation of finitude and estrangement, sharing our human condition even unto death. Just as empathy descends into the depths of the hell and alienation of the partner, so, according to Christian memory, does God descend into the hell of human estrangement to be there with his redemptive presence and power. Just as the intimate enters the frame of reference of his partner and participates in his struggle, so God, according to Christian witness, participates concretely in our human estrangement without himself being estranged. The analogy has its limits, of course, since human empathy is not infinite empathy. The human capacity to understand is short of, though it may partially reflect, God's understanding.)[29]

Congruence. The next aspect of intimacy is closely related to empathy. It has to do with each partner's capacity to feel *his own* feelings. The technical term for this is congruence, which means that I am in touch with my own experiencing process, fully self-aware. To the degree that I experience my own feelings as they actually are and do not protect myself against having them, intimacy will be increased. Let us suppose that I have learned to block not only from my partner's awareness but from my own awareness certain uncomfortable experiences (shaded in the above diagram). It will make it all the more difficult for my partner to understand them empathetically. If I am so out of touch with myself that important experiences are not accessible even to me, then it will not be easy for my inner life to be shared, and thus will block intimacy.

Trained as we are by lengthy acculturation *not* to feel certain negative feelings, notably anger, many persons in our culture find that it is difficult to open their experiencing process to another. Persons who have difficulty coming close to themselves have difficulty coming close to others.

Congruence is defined by Rogers as a condition in which "self-experiences are accurately symbolized, and are included in the self-concept in this accurately symbolized form."[30] The intimate is congruent when he feels his feelings clearly, is fully aware of his present experiencing, and symbolizes his feelings adequately.

EMOTIVE WARMTH AND CONFLICT CAPABILITY

If the relationship is essentially warm and affirming, must not it necessarily be forced into conflict-avoidance?

I answer with our fourth irony: It is precisely the intimacy most deeply nourished by affection that is most capable of constructive conflict or "fair fighting."[31] Stated concisely, *the intimate relationship is emotively warm, yet conflict-capable.*

Surely the most recognizable aspect of intimacy is emotive warmth. The fact that such warmth can sometimes get "hot" amid conflicting interests constitutes a special problem of the intimate relationship. Here the work of George Bach[32] has been most useful. He rightly notes that hostility is a closer relationship than indifference. An angry scene may be much more intimate than one characterized by boredom or innocuousness.

Bach correctly reminds us that genuinely intimate partners are more than less likely to fight. Bach tries to teach partners to fight fair instead of dirty. The assumption is that any close relationship is going to be conflicted from time to time, and that if you can teach partners to fight openly, candidly, and without manipulative ploys, then the chances are increased that intimacy will not only survive but deepen through the conflict.[33]

Thus while it is true that acceptance and affection are essential ingredients in intimacy, it is not necessary for them to be constant or syrupy. Deep intimacy can break into open hostility provided partners are able to look honestly at conflicted interests and frustrations, and work through them together with confidence in each other's basic trustworthiness.[34]

A relationship wholly devoid of any warm flow of positive affect or affirmation would hardly be called intimate. Intimacy is, according to the arcane language of transactional analysis, the "best way to get strokes," the ultimately satisfying form of stroking, beyond games and pastimes.[35]

Intimates sometimes report experiencing what seems to be an unconditional positive regard precisely amid their inconsistencies and compulsions, so as to liberate them to feel more fully their actual feelings in the presence of the other. Although the partner's positive regard is never finally unconditional, in the most serious sense, nevertheless at times the intimate experiences it as unconditional. Orthodox Christian thought beholds in such seemingly unconditional human love a mirror or reflection of the unconditional love of God.[36]

Readers familiar with the psychotherapeutic tradition will notice that I have just used another therapeutic term (or construct employed by certain therapists) to describe intimacy, namely, unconditional positive regard (or UPR). Rogers describes UPR as "a warm caring . . . which is not possessive, which demands no personal gratification. It is an atmosphere which simply demonstrates 'I care'; not 'I care for you if you behave thus and so[37]." It is a "prizing" which functions without "conditions of worth."

No one can achieve such an attitude simply by willing it or wishing it were so. The profound prizing of the other without conditions is not readily manufacturable, and must emerge somehow from the wellsprings of one's philosophical orientation and character structure.[38] But at least the recipient of UPR knows, when he experiences it, that it opens up the door internally for greater risk, wider openness, clearer congruence, deeper self-disclosure, and consequently greater intimacy. Why? Because when I experience myself in the presence of one who truly prizes my very being without placing conditions on me, I experience a new freedom to feel those feelings that would be far too dangerous in a more conditional setting.[39]

Thus persons in such intimate relationships often report feeling relatively *safe* with the other. They do not feel that they need to defend themselves. There may be continuing needs for security operations, but in the intimate moment the demand for them is sharply reduced.

A related characteristic of intimacy is tactile or bodily closeness. From time to time the affectionate relationship wishes to manifest itself in touching. The spirit relation or psychological closeness of persons becomes naturally embodied in a touch relationship.[40]

We do well not to stress this point so compulsively as to appear to make it necessary at all or most times for intimacies to be body transactions. But while it is not a necessary condition, tactile intimacy may be at times the most fitting expression of close companionship. Friends embrace, even though an embrace does not constitute friendship. Lovers make love, even though orgasm does not constitute intimacy. The significance of touch relationships differ widely, of course, from culture to culture.

Can we assume honesty as an absolute norm of the intimate relationship without coercively requiring self-disclosure?

The hypothesis that holds together this fifth tension or irony is: *An intimate relationship is honest, open, nondeceptive, game-free, nonmanipulative, and self-disclosing, and yet it does not compulsively require of the partner self-disclosure and petty acts of confession and compulsive honesty.* It allows the partner, when appropriate, distance, solitude, autonomy, and self-direction.[41]

The Hebraic commandment, "Thou shalt not bear false witness against thy neighbor," is the most elemental norm of personal intimacy.[42] Yet within the framework of truth-telling, intimacy leaves room for a certain "letting be", the allowing of the partner to be who he is.

Emphasis on intimacy as nonmanipulative calls to mind the special definition of intimacy proposed by the transactional analysts; namely, that intimacy is a "game-free relationship." Berne defines intimacy as "a game free exchange of emotional expression without exploitation."[43] Intimacy, according to James and Jongeward, is "free of games and free of exploitation."[44] Although this may at first appear to be merely defining intimacy negatively in terms of something that is absent from it, nonetheless when one remembers the exceptional specificity given to the notion of games by the transactional analysts, the definition takes on more substance.

It is in this frame of reference that we note another condition or characteristic of intimacy: the capacity for self-disclosure. It is the willingness to reveal oneself, to open one's internal knowledge to the view of the other. Jourard[45] has paid special attention to the function of self-disclosure in therapeutic growth. Whereas behaviorist and Freudian psychologies had presupposed that persons resist self-disclosure, and thus devise deceptive experiments and stratagems to break through resistance, Jourard's studies found to the contrary that persons in an accepting environment positively *desire* self-disclosure. Thus therapy is not merely a matter of coercively breaking through resistances, but rather allowing the conditions that permit individuals to reveal what is within. Such conditions facilitate intimacy.

Since the quality of emotive communication is so decisive for intimacy, further attention needs to be given to defining just what we mean by it. The intimate relationship is characterized by an emotive resonance, the nuances of which are admirably evoked in the colloquial image of "good vibes." Intimates experience many subtle energy vibrations between each other, i.e., many signals both verbal and nonverbal that the partner picks up quickly and unmistakably. Just because there are so many transmissions of this sort, both sensory and parasensory, it is virtually impossible for intimates to lie to each other, since their body language and aura perceptions tell the truth, as studies of affairs have shown.[46] Persons having affairs have unaccustomed difficulty telling lies to intimates. The person with whom one is or has long been intimate picks up the nonverbal and etheric signals beyond all verbal concealments.

Even though honesty is a crucial virtue of intimates, they nonetheless find it prudent not to coerce honesty, nor to compel each other to be compulsively self-disclosing. Intimacy must give room for being oneself. It must allow distance, when distance means growth or survival. Intimacy is not an undermining of individuality but an enhancement of it.[47] If the relation is compulsively controlling and the companion is not allowed to shape his own direction, then the mutual respect that intimacy requires is inhibited.[48]

It may seem paradoxical to suggest that intimacy and solitude are mutually supportive, since solitude may at first glance appear to be the mirror opposite of intimacy. Yet, as our discussion of empathy and congruence has shown, one can be more free to be in touch with others if he is in touch with himself. Thus a rhythm of intimacy and solitude appears to be supportive to both.[49]

FINITUDE AND TRANSCENDENCE

Is intimacy subject to death, or does it transcend death? In a later chapter I will deal more explicitly with finitude and spirit in interpersonal communion. But for now the essential dialectic can be concisely stated in two phases: intimacy as finite and intimacy as self-transcending.

Finitude. Since intimacy is a relationship that exists in history and thus within the context of human finitude, it is subject to death. It is a misunderstanding of the intimate relationship to pretend that it lacks limits. For each time I commit myself to a relation of closeness to another person I take the risk of losing it. It is only wise to realize that any human bonding is vulnerable to deterioration, sickness, loss, and finally death.

Although one might suppose that modern scientific empiricism would have little difficulty in grasping and affirming this thesis, that is not so evident. For there appears to be just as strong a temptation among modern men to make an idolatry of the interpersonal as in more primitive cultures, to treat the finite relationship as if it were absolute or not subject to time and death. This is a basic dilemma in all human existence: the temptation to take a finite good and deal with it as if it were the whole good, to absolutize the relative.[50]

To the extent that we idolize finite intimacy, we make ourselves vulnerable to the pain over its loss. The nature of intimacy is best served not by idolizing the intimate partner, but by dealing with the intimate realistically as a person subject to death, so that the relation can develop with an awareness of its actual fragility and lack of absoluteness in time.

Transcendence. The other side of the dialectic that deepens the irony is that interpersonal communion characteristically understands itself (when it understands itself deeply) as transcending the finite sphere, and as touching or being touched by the eternal Other through interpersonal meeting.[51] Interpersonal existence is from time to time sharply aware of itself as rooted in the inner meaning of the cosmos. This widely known experience leads us to hypothesize that intimacy, though gravely subject to finitude and death, nonetheless transcends it in mysterious ways that are not fully capable at this time of empirical verification.

Instead of defensively trying to fashion a statement on interpersonal transcendence that would be acceptable to a rigid reductive naturalism, my own inclination is to state this last point confessionally. The Christian hope beholds and celebrates interpersonal existence from the vantage point of its end, that is, its conclusion at the end of history. It is an audacious assumption of Christian faith that the end of history is in some sense already revealed.[52] Christian hope acts as though it knew the essential direction of history, even though admittedly the historical process is painfully incomplete.

If resurrection is personal, it is interpersonal. If the Judeo-Christian hope for the future is a hope for human renewal, then it is a hope for the renewal of the interpersonal life beyond death. Such renewal may be a transmuted form of life far different or beyond that which we can now envision with our limited sensory mechanisms. Paul himself seems to have envisioned such a transmutation when he wrote, "For not all flesh is alike, but there is one kind for men, another for animals, another for birds, and another for fish. . . . So it is with the resurrection of the dead. What is sown is perishable, what is raised is imperishable. . . . It is sown a physical body, it is raised a spiritual body" (1 Corinthians 15:39–44).

Intimates are aware that their most significant exchanges are not merely body transactions, but as persons in encounter, or the meeting of spirit with spirit. What really happens in intimacy has to do with spirit-spirit communion or interpersonal communion, two persons experiencing their beings poignantly united. When they are most together they are most aware of that which transcends their togetherness. Their oneness reflects a deeper capacity for coherence in the universe. Their interpersonal communion echoes some abyssal capacity given in and with reality itself for communion.

It may be more useful to summarize these twelve points by stating them negatively, rather than positively.

1. Intimate relationships do not grow if not given time.

2. Intimate bonding is less palpable if it never has ways of becoming intensified into ecstatic moments of intimate sharing.

3. If relationships lack contractual clarity, or if the contracts are easily terminable, then to that degree the relationship is less intimate-capable.

4. If within the framework of sustained accountability the relationship is not able to be renegotiated in the light of specific new demands and occasions, then it is less likely to be intimate.

5. If partners are unable to empathize with each other's feelings, intimacy is inhibited.

6. If persons are unable to feel their own feelings clearly and fully,

then the empathy that intimacy requires is constricted.

7. If emotive warmth is absent consistently, one is not likely to call the relation intimate.

8. Relationships that are unable to face conflicts are less likely to develop intimacy.

9. Insofar as partners need to resort to deceptive and manipulative behaviors, or lack honest self-disclosure, the relationship is to that degree probably less intimate.

10. To the extent that the relationship requires the constant monitoring of one party and thus inhibits the self-direction of the other, intimacy is decreased.

11. Insofar as the relationship is not recognized as finite and therefore vulnerable to death, it is less likely to achieve genuine intimacy, since it will be prone to idolize the partner.

12. And yet intimates know that when they are most together they are most aware of that which transcends their togetherness, echoing the abysmal capacity given in and with reality itself for communion. It is this experience that energizes the hope that intimacy, in some mysterious way not fully explainable at this time, transcends death.

This attempt at a conceptual clarification of the notion of intimacy has one special difficulty. As we proceed to define intimacy we easily tend to become burdened by a highly idealized picture of the intimate relationship, so that it seems increasingly abstract and impossible to grasp as an actual or even potential reality. It is not necessary for all factors to be present in their absolute form in order for a relation to be intimate. Any one of these factors may have its ebbs and flows. But over a period of time if these conditions tend to persist in a relation between two persons, then they experience that special relation to which our common language points when it uses the term intimacy.

Having discussed the language, the collage of descriptions and the ironies of the intimate relationship, I am now ready to offer a definition of intimacy. *Intimacy is an intensely personal relationship of sustained closeness in which the intimus sphere of each partner is affectionately known and beheld by the other through congruent, empathic understand-*

ing, mutual accountability, and contextual negotiability, durable in time, subject to ecstatic intensification, emotively warm and conflict-capable, self-disclosing and distance-respecting, subject to death and yet in the form of hope reaching beyond death.

2. Dilemmas of Intimacy

Having established a working definition of intimacy, I am now able to examine some of the reasons why persons so desperately resist intimacy; and to explore reasons why the sexualized hunger for intimacy in our culture is similar to the thirst for salvation in previous religiously oriented cultures.

The Hazards of the Intimate Relationship

Thus far it might appear that intimacy is a wholly desirable experience, with few risks or perplexities. But not all intimacy is growth-producing, renewing, or pleasant. It can be terrifying, parasitical, and malignant. Why is it that approaching closeness awakens in so many such desperate anxieties and resistance?

A truly close relationship may be a painful and demanding crucible. Sometimes when we get closest to the inner reality of a partner, we find ourselves increasingly vulnerable to his or her compulsive needs, tragic flaws, and destructive possibilities.[1]

Intimacy involves us in a tangled web of accountability that many are happy to avoid. A relation lacking accountability is not likely to be very intimate. Yet we may pay dearly for sustained mutual accountability.

Genuine friendship may require partners to be radically responsive at unexpected times to sickness, crisis, or emergency. And there are times when nothing is more important. At such times I must adjust my schedule of priorities without reference to my needs or interests, just as I would hope that my friend would respond to me in actual need.

It is foolish to imagine that we can enter close relationships without cost. Some people understandably would prefer to live in relative isolation rather than take on the potentially burdensome responsibilities of intimacy.[2]

I may have difficulty mustering the empathy necessary to be an intimate partner. I may be so preoccupied with my own needs and blockages that it is very difficult for me simply to listen to someone else.[3] It may take enormous amounts of psychological energy to really enter into another's feeling processes. Thus I may intuitively realize that it is much better at a particular time not to get trapped in a relationship where that sort of empathy would be expected or desired. I may have to protect myself against easily disappointable expectations.

I may put up stiff resistance to intense closeness out of fear of self-disclosure. I fear I might get caught in a situation in which my vulnerabilities might be too painfully evident, both to others and myself.[4] I might have become long habituated to deception, and thus know intuitively that when another comes close to me, my knavery or disingenuousness might be grossly revealed. My mask of respectability might be taken away. So I keep my distance, protect myself from closeness, and scare anyone away who seems ready to draw near.

I may have found that my habits of manipulation will get me the things I want through the very kinds of control that destroy or hamper intimacy. I recognize correctly that if I get into an intimate relationship those manipulative and controlling functions might have to be sharply curbed in order to enable intimacy. That could be a high price.

Further, I may find it very difficult to be in touch with my own experiencing process in such a way as to be self-revealing. I may be internally blocked and defensive. I may not feel like opening up those blocks at a particular time. For if I expose those vulnerable parts to myself, much less to another, I dread that my security system might be destroyed or I might be conned by another untrustworthy potential intimate.

I may value my independence too much to relate intimately. I may be at a point in my own history, quite legitimately, in which I am struggling to gain the "courage to be as oneself"[5] (which Tillich distinguished from the "courage to be as a part," namely, the courage to be independent, to rely on myself). In those moments, I may feel that I need intimacy less than solitude. I may hunger for the chance to reintegrate myself and feel my feelings alone, and to give myself a rest from excessive or debilitating closeness. I may need distance for independent growth. There may be periods, even long periods, in which I prefer a certain withdrawal or moratorium on close relationships.[6] Both body and spirit at times hunger to be alone.

People spurn intimacy in order to fight wars, make money, create works of art, win votes, spark revolutions, etc. All of these pursuits may be regarded as of higher value or situational urgency than person-to-person intimacy.

Intimate relationships are limited by time. Persons may reject the intimate relationship because they are in the process of doing other things that seem to them contextually more obligatory or pleasurable than intimacy.

Lack of time, of course, may become a convenient excuse for not building relationships when the real reasons may be the more substantial ones I have already indicated. But intimacy does take time. Some would rather not pay that price.

At the risk of becoming too self-referential, I use myself as an example of the temporal limits of intimacy. I am committed to many time-consuming involvements that fall into shifting orders of priorities: family, teaching, civic responsibilities, home maintenance, being a neighbor, a friend, a bookkeeper, a colleague, a scholar, a voter, etc. Few things are more important to me than relationships of closeness: with family, students, friends, and colleagues. Yet this does not change the fact that other subpersonal and intrapersonal values persistently place decisive claims upon me. Most days I find that I have to rule out options that would bring me close to some persons in order to be closer to others or to actualize impersonal values. Choice demands negation.[7]

I am discovering that I have only a limited capacity for intimacy. It is possible for me to be close to a few persons but not to many. Even with these few, my capacity for intimacy depends on my energy level, interest of the moment, available time, and the current posture of my security needs.

It is asking far too much of intimacy to assume it as a normative permanent condition. That is not the shape of the interpersonal sphere as I experience it. Nonintimate, lower priority, yet necessary demands such as paying bills, maintaining a modest standard of order and cleanliness, answering correspondence, buying supplies, preparing for assumed responsibilities, and innumerable nonpersonal routine activities must also be done. So, although I desire intimacy, I also desire and feel obligated to pursue other values that compete with intimate relationships for time and energy.

It may be that a person finds that he is getting enough strokes from achievement, games, activities, or pastimes without intimacy, or even if he does exist in a stroke deficit, he still might feel that there are ways of getting strokes in a less risky way than through intimacy, e.g., through earning praise or recognition. There must be plausible reasons why so many persons seem to prefer deceptive games to intimacy. Their judgment must not prejudicially be assumed to be nonsensical or unworthy of the human spirit.[8]

Others may reject a potential intimacy on behalf of another intimate. Spouses, for instance, often rule out potential intimates of the other sex in order to reinforce and not confuse their sexual commitment to the spouse. Choice demands negation.

Finally there is the possibility that the close relationship will be taken away by death or the accidents of history. Anticipatory grief causes persons to resist intimacy, and for very good reasons. When persons have become aware that the intimate relationships in which they may have deeply invested themselves have been swept away instantly by death, they may think twice about another such risk.

All relationships are vulnerable to separation, sickness, rejection, social change, revolution, war, and above all death. Grief feelings can occur in many situations short of, but usually analogous to, death. Time, distance, human willing, and the uncertainties of human history make all relationships vulnerable.

Any time another person becomes for me a center of value[9] (a value in terms of which I judge other values to be valuable), then I make myself vulnerable to the grief-laden loss of that center of value (which the Hebraic tradition called, perhaps harshly, a "god," an idol, a finite value absolutized yet subject to destruction). Persons who unwisely invest total energies in a single intimacy often find upon the death of their partner a diffuse sense of meaninglessness and a need for considerable personal redefinition. Grief is a profound instructor. The relationship was deeply valuable; now it is gone. It cannot be given up without painful feelings of separation from a central source of value. Life is not the same without the intimate.[10]

Some who have been through that grief or something analogous to it may not wish to suffer it again. Understandable questions following grief are: Shall I ever allow myself to become so vulnerable again? Shall I ever let myself be so deeply enmeshed in the life of another person that I give myself the possibility of being so hurt again?

There are persons who survive long periods of time without intimacy of almost any sort. That is a condition I can only describe as loneliness. In this state, one experiences his inner life as not being shared, even if others are physically nearby. No one else is in touch with one's *intimum*. There is minimal affection or empathy in one's meetings with others.[11]

Many people rightly intuit eminent danger in close relationships. They know they can be hurt quickly, deeply, and perhaps irreparably. I want to respect those who stay out of intimacy. They may feel the need simply to survive as separate individuals. They may have been so deeply injured by dehumanizing intimacies that they are quite certain they will never get so entangled again.

Nonetheless, having admitted this possibility, it still remains that many persons who have in fact taken these risks and ventured out into the arduous, costly, painful realm of interpersonal intimacy, although they may come back with scars, bruises, grief, and various problems, still answer clearly that only in intimacy have they discovered the deeper meaning of their lives. Only there in the affectionate closeness of bonding with another have they discovered their own deepest identity, been able to celebrate the depths of human existence, grasped life as coherent, and sensed their participation in the inner meaning of the cosmos.

So it is not my intention to commend without qualification the intimate life-style for everyone, or suggest that it can be sought to the neglect of legitimate competing values. But as is often true in the human enterprise, the greater the risk, the greater the possibility of enrichment. And so it seems with intimacy.

Closer Than Sex

I want to be explicit and straightforward about one viewpoint against which I am struggling: the subtle or overt assumption that intimacy is essentially sexual closeness.[12] I regret that so many modern men and women have become trapped in the twisted assumption that intimacy is reducible to coital scoring. It has become a widely popular post-Freudian miscalculation that if you make it in sexual relationships you have made it in interpersonal relationships. The whole tenor and drift of my argument is in tension with this popular assumption, which regrettably has been fostered by bogus psychology and phony "experts" on "human encounter."

Recently a male lion who had become famous for his sexual potency died in a California zoo. This elderly lion was given elaborate funeral rites and honored as an object of social admiration. It is amusing, although not surprising, that a culture seeking salvation through sex would choose a sexually active elderly lion as a culture hero, a choice almost wholly unimaginable a few decades ago.

I have already indicated that the theme of intimacy is historically and linguistically connected with sexuality, and for very good reasons, since intimacy speaks of closeness to others, and for many the human experience that best epitomizes human closeness is genital sexuality.

The post-Freudian period has rightly taught us that sexual closeness is an important aspect of human fulfillment, but wrongly and excessively told us that our human fulfillment depends almost frantically and unilaterally on sexual fulfillment,[13] so much so in fact that many are engaged in a desperate search for sexual gratification that sometimes takes on the nuances of a crusade or gnostic mystery rite or pietistic revival meeting. Sex is the new salvation quest.[14]

It is precisely the urgent and demanding character of this sexual quest that reduces actual and potential intimacy. There is an ironic point of no return at which the quest for sexual fulfillment becomes manipulative and defeats its own deepest intention (closeness with another). Literally millions of men and women have suffered through the demoralizing results of these assumptions. They have been exploited by spurious pop "therapies" and pseudopsychologies.[15]

I am going to invent a term (something I normally dislike others to do), a word to describe something I cannot find in my dictionary: *anorgasmophobia* (literally, lacking orgasm fear). It means a phobic response to sexual inactivity, the dread of not having an orgasm today. It emerges out of a heavy *ought*, the normative assumption that everyone ought to be "sexually healthy" and thus regularly active sexually. The demoralization and anxiety we post-Freudians feel when we are sexually indolent or laggard may be called *anorgasmophobic* (or, if you wish to anglicize it, simply asexophobic). The Masters and Johnson[16] and other sex clinics are responses to this culture-conditioned phobia, the fear of the absence of the very sexuality that has come to represent salvation of the psyche (soul) from the hell of sexual inactivity.

The sex clinics tend to function with the same messianic quality found in second-century gnosticism. There a secret knowledge was being passed on in an arcane way from teachers to practitioners. If and when catacumens learned the secret words, procedures, and rituals, they could then be transported to the ecstasies of the primal light world. Just as some forms of gnosticism became a manipulative escapism, so can sexual redemptionism become an escape from the sustained demands of responsible intimacy.[17]

This fear is endemic to post-Freudian society. In no other society than excessively psychologized post-Freudian America does human fulfillment presumably hinge so directly and compulsively on frenetic sexual activism. It is hard to imagine any other society suffering widespread distress because of anorgasmophobia. Under these conditions, the real test case of interpersonal competence is assumed to be sexual competence. Carried to its logical extreme, interpersonal happiness is equated with genital proclivities, and little else.

This temptation to reduce interpersonal encounter to sexual encounter has, I believe, yielded untold misery in our culture.[18] Admittedly all personal relationships have sexual nuances, but the perimeters of personal relationships can hardly be defined by sexuality. While there are no nonsexual forms of human relationship—since persons are by definition sexual—it is time to resist the popular tendency to reduce personal interaction to sexual interaction.[19] While coitus is one of the most evident models for personal closeness, it is not more profound than the Hebraic model of responsible covenant fidelity.

Our common expectation that sex is the closest human relationship may be misconceived. Sex may be alienating to intimacy as well as enabling of it. Sex without interpersonal intimacy is like a diploma without an education. Intimacy is closer than sex.

Far from putting down sexuality, I am arguing that sexuality belongs within and is best fulfilled in the environment of intimacy—a statement both very traditional and very change-oriented in the post-Freudian context.

3. Therapy as Surrogate Intimacy

How does the preceding definition of intimacy correlate with recent research on psychotherapeutic effectiveness?

The Hypothesis

What happens in therapy? What kind of relationship is offered in effective psychotherapy that elicits growth, heals the broken fabric of personality, and allays phobic responses, guilt, and demoralization?

It was not until I had proceeded deeply into my study of intimacy that I even raised the question of its analogies with therapy. Then I realized that much of the language being used to describe intimacy was precisely that most often used to describe the therapeutic process. It focused suddenly for me that much of what is called "therapeutic effectiveness" may actually be better described as an attempt to provide a relationship that will simulate the conditions of intimacy.

Among the characteristics of intimacy that are also widely acknowledged components of the therapeutic relationship are accurate empathy, nonpossessive warmth, congruence, self-disclosure, unconditional positive regard, openness, genuineness, and contractual clarity. Researchers who have in fact attempted to describe clinically the necessary and sufficient conditions of therapeutic effectiveness have often cited just these characteristics.[1]

Thus I am led to propose and will present evidence to support the view that therapeutic effectiveness, regardless of theoretical orientation, is essentially a surrogate intimacy, a substitute that is needed when the real thing is not there. Surrogate, in my meaning, does not imply phony, artificial, unreal or worthless. Many of the richest conditions of intimacy are in fact present in therapy. What is not present is a sustained relation of broad-ranging mutual accountability.

However similar, therapy and intimacy are not the same. They can be analogous only if they are in some ways different. They differ in that the relationship in therapy is purchased. Persons are accountable at a certain level but not beyond the limits of the therapeutic contract, in which the therapist agrees to try to provide therapeutic conditions for a fee. The therapist understandably resists doing more than what the fee covers; intimacy goes further. Therapy is basically a skeletal image of intimacy that has become professionalized.

Therapy is quite evidently similar to intimacy in its sphere of special concern. That which is *intimus* is in fact the particular sphere of therapy. The therapist has as his task the reaching of that inmost feeling level, affect level, the hidden *intimum* of the person, knowing it, resonating with it, working to heal it.

I do not wish to overstate this thesis so as to suggest that therapists are trying to create relationships of intimacy. Most therapists do not understand themselves in that way and many would resist the assertion that therapy is a surrogate intimacy. But the kind of relationship that develops, nonetheless, has many of the central characteristics of intimacy, as the clinical evidence that I will present will show.

It might at first seem that therapy is quite unlike intimacy, for intimacy ordinarily requires a duration of time to take root and deepen. But therapists often remind their clients that improvement will take time, often much time. In its need for time to develop interpersonal sensitivity and emotive resonance, psychotherapy is similar to intimacy. It takes the time to get in touch with the *intimus* sphere of another.

A therapeutic relationship, when effective, is characteristically able to dig into the stress points where the client is conflicted. The Freudian notion of transference illustrates particularly well the point of *conflict-*

capability in therapy. For essential to the dynamics of therapy, according to Freud, is a "transference relationship" in which one works through distortions in the relation to his therapist in ways that are analogous to earlier conflicts with significant others.[2] The relation often becomes highly conflicted. Thus therapy is conflict-capable, again like intimacy.

Szasz and Berne both deal with accountability between client and therapist in describing the therapeutic contract. They argue that when a person finds himself in a well-functioning therapeutic relation, he is in the presence of a person who is thoroughly accountable to him within the limits of the therapeutic contract.[3] Contractual clarity is essential to the therapeutic as well as the intimate relationship.

Yet in intimacy there is no clear fixed, specific terminus to the term of accountability, whereas in psychotherapy there is always assumed to be an intended terminus, when symptoms disappear and the client no longer needs therapeutic services. The contract will, unlike intimacy, be terminated.

Thus the therapeutic relationship offers to the intimacy-deprived or intimacy-victimized person many of the conditions of genuine intimacy, conditions that are present in fact in all authentic interpersonal communion, and in any open, honest, responsible, caring, personal relationship. It is no wonder that Berne says that "love . . . is nature's psychotherapy."[4]

The Supportive Evidence

To develop this thesis, I will introduce evidence that will question the overrated efficaciousness of *average* psychotherapy; define *effective* psychotherapy, indicating its correlation with the conditions of intimacy;[5] and report outcomes of a recent study in "structured intimacy."

AVERAGE PSYCHOTHERAPY AND SPONTANEOUS REMISSION RATES

There is mounting evidence that average professional psychotherapy is not nearly as effective as most therapists and their clients have imagined. In the early 1950s, H. J. Eysenck[6] presented statistical evidence that psychotherapy on the average is no better than spontaneous remission rates, or rates of improvement achieved simply through the passing of time. After an extensive review of the relevant literature on therapeutic outcomes since 1952, Truax and Carkhuff (1967) concluded that "Eysenck was essentially correct in saying that *average* counseling and psychotherapy as it is currently practiced does not result in average client improvement greater than that observed in clients who received no special counseling or psychotherapeutic treatment."[7]

Other studies support this conclusion. In *Persuasion and Healing* (1961), Jerome Frank noted that the improvement rate for patients receiving psychotherapy was about two-thirds, but that same rate was found for comparable patients who had no psychotherapy.[8] A study by Barron and Leary (1955) of 150 neurotic patients who were tested before and after treatment on MMPI neuroticism scales showed no significant differences in improvement among individuals who had received group psychotherapy, individual psychotherapy, and no psychotherapy.[9] Similarly, in separate studies comparing spontaneous remission rates to rates of improvement under psychotherapy by Cartwright and Vogel (1960), Mink and Isaacson (1959), Gliedman, Nash, Imber, Stone, and Frank (1958), Walker and Kelley (1960), and Barendregt (1961), no overall differences in outcome were reported in favor of those receiving psychotherapy.[10] Anker and Walsh (1961) studied improvement rates among hospitalized patients receiving group therapy as compared with drama group activity, and found consistently greater improvement for the drama group than those in therapy.[11]

Despite all of this negative evidence, a continuing momentum of confidence persists among therapists that any therapy will likely be better than none, and that their therapeutic skills are worthy of the client's trust, fees, and the whole apparatus of professional confidence.

Furthermore, on the basis of studies by Levitt (1957), Eysenck (1960), Mink and Isaacson (1959), and others,[12] *"the evidence now available suggests that, on the average, psychotherapy may be harmful as often as helpful, with an average effect comparable to receiving no help."*[13]

Similarly, Allen Bergin (1971) concludes his exhaustive evaluation of over two hundred studies of therapeutic outcomes with a plea for a moratorium on "a large proportion of the traditional therapy currently practiced." "Our faith is that whatever is powerful in traditional therapy resides in the work of a minority of its practitioners . . . there is little reason to reinforce or reassure the ordinary practitioner of psychotherapy, for we expect future research to show that his labors must be revised toward matching the behavior of a few successful peers who actually obtain most of the therapeutic results."[14]

Thus the populist critique of average psychotherapy[15] is beginning to be supported by substantial clinical evidence. As we approach the analogy of therapy and intimacy, we cannot assume any substantiated confidence in the effectiveness of psychotherapy professionally.

RESEARCH CONSENSUS ON THERAPEUTIC EFFECTIVENESS

There is a growing body of research that supports the hypothesis that at least three conditions present in intimacy are also crucial and in fact definitive for the therapeutic relationship: accurate empathy, nonpossessive warmth, and genuiness. This so-called therapeutic triad is found repeatedly in a broad range of research into therapeutic effectiveness. This consensus has been formulated by Truax and Carkhuff on the basis of substantial research by therapists of widely differing theoretical orientations. These three factors correspond generally with the Rogerian terms for "the necessary and sufficient conditions of therapeutic personality change": empathy, congruence, and unconditional positive regard.[16]

Lest this all seem like exaggerated personal opinion, I will briefly summarize some studies which show that the ingredients of effective therapeutic agency are definable, that therapeutic results may be achieved by persons who have had no formal training in developmental psychology and psychotherapy, and that many of the ingredients repeatedly mentioned as essential elements of therapeutic effectiveness are precisely the ingredients of our essential definition of intimacy.

A substantial body of evidence exists to indicate that persons who are

accurately empathetic, nonpossessively warm in attitude, and genuine are indeed effective; the greater the degree to which these elements were present in the therapeutic encounter, the greater was the resulting constructive personality change. . . . These findings seem to hold for a wide variety of therapists and counselors *regardless of their training or theoretic orientation;* and for a wide variety of clients or patients, including college underachievers, juvenile delinquents, hospitalized schizophrenics, college counselors, mild to severe outpatient neurotics, and the mixed variety of hospitalized patients. Further, the evidence suggests that these findings hold in a variety of therapeutic contexts and in both individual and group psychotherapy or counseling.[17]

There is considerable evidence for this conclusion. A Johns Hopkins study by Whitehorn and Betz compared seven well-functioning psychiatrists whose schizophrenic patient improvement was 75 percent with seven other poorly rated psychiatrists of similar training whose improvement rate was only 27 percent. The differences in therapists were not in theoretical orientation or training but in attitudinal and relational styles. Betz's (1963) descriptions of these successful therapists were consistent with the triad that appears so frequently in major theoretical formulations of effective therapy: empathic understanding, nonpossessive warmth, and authenticity.[18]

One of the most extensive clinical studies of the conditions of therapeutic effectiveness is the Wisconsin Schizophrenic Project, in which many eminent leaders were involved, including Truax, Rogers, Wargo, Carkhuff, Gendlin, and others.

Patients had been randomly assigned to either therapy or control conditions within the matched pairs, and a complete battery of psychological tests was given initially and later. The therapy patients received a minimum of 30 individual therapy sessions and a maximum of 280 sessions throughout a three and one-half year period. . . . Samples of tape-recorded interviews were independently rated for therapist accurate empathy, nonpossessive warmth, and genuineness. . . . The findings indicated that patients receiving high levels of the three conditions showed an overall gain in psychological functioning; but those patients who received rather low levels showed a *loss* in psychological functioning.[19]

Research procedures have even been designed to measure the therapeutic triad and assess its levels among lay persons as compared with professionals. The results were remarkable. They compared levels of therapeutic effectiveness of lay persons to postgraduate clinical psychology trainees, and then to a group of experienced therapists, such as Carl Whitaker, Rollo May, Albert Ellis, and Carl Rogers.

After slightly less than 100 hours of training . . . the levels of accurate empathy communicated to patients were not significantly different between the three groups . . . there were no significant differences between the three groups in terms of the level of nonpossessive warmth. . . . With respect to therapist's genuineness, however, the experienced therapists showed a significantly higher level of genuineness or self-congruence than did the lay trainees. . . . The level of patient depth of self-exploration achieved in therapy did not differ significantly between the three groups. . . . These data suggest that these ingredients can be learned, by both professional and nonprofessional persons.[20]

This evidence supports the hypothesis that what distinguishes effective psychotherapy from average (noneffective) psychotherapy is the presence of these three conditions of the therapeutic triad, which are also present in the intimate relationship.

Further research showed that when persons who ordinarily are nonempathic, hostile, and defensive (i.e., lacking in the therapeutic triad), were able to learn to communicate these three elements in a therapy hour, they would still be relatively more effective than average therapists.

The currently available evidence, then, suggests that these ingredients of accurate empathy, nonpossessive warmth and therapist genuineness are "teachable"; and that even nonprofessional persons lacking expert knowledge of psychopathology and personality dynamics can, under supervision, produce positive changes in chronic hospitalized patient populations.[21]

This leads us to serious questions about the viability of psychotherapeutic professionalization. For can the intimate relationship be professionalized? Can the conditions and characteristics of intimacy be offered adequately under the limitations of a fee-paying relationship? Does not the professional relationship itself mitigate against the offering of those therapeutic conditions? This is not a question we can expect psychotherapists to raise enthusiastically, influenced as they understandably are by professional self-interest. The question is a difficult one. In *After Therapy What?*,[22] I have already begun to explore this dilemma. The problem is in fact intensified by these analogies between intimacy and effective psychotherapy.

The most thoroughgoing study of the function of companionship in therapy is Gerald Goodman's *Companionship Therapy: Studies in Structured Intimacy,* which reports an attempt to provide a therapeutic relationship by nonprofessional "companions" under controlled conditions with carefully built-in processes for evaluation.

The companionship format was motivated by the need for new manpower in the mental health field, especially in the light of eroding confidence in the medical practitioner model. Researchers viewed the entry of nonprofessionals into the sphere of therapeutic change as a logical phase in the history of mental health economics. Historic precedents may be found in Alcoholics Anonymous, Synanon, Big Brothers, and more recently the Esalen-oriented growth centers, integrity therapy groups, transactional analysis groups, etc.[23]

The "troubled boys" who were the subjects of this study were characterized as "unmanageable mischief-makers who demanded attention, created disorder, felt restless, and lacked friends . . . all the observer groups saw our samples as troubled."[24] University students were employed as companions. The study included a design for measuring the companionship process. The process lasted for four years in various phases.

In measuring the effectiveness of companionship, the primary variables were "understanding (empathy), openness (self-disclosure), and acceptance-warmth, which combine to form a therapeutic talent composite"[25] (again, the therapeutic triad):

Each of the necessary and sufficient conditions of therapeutic personality change formulated by Rogers (1957) can be seen, in less obvious fashion, in everyday behavior—in the person regarded as a good listener, who understands the other person's feelings; in the person regarded as spontaneous, open, "straight," self-disclosing; or in the person described as having an accepting nature. A few unusual people possess these traits in combination. We wanted to find people with these combined traits.[26]

Thus Goodman specifically looked for lay persons who had already developed these conditions of the therapeutic triad. Further, he developed a procedure by which he could score levels of the therapeutic triad in companionship counselors, the Group Assessment of Interpersonal Traits (GAIT), which identified individuals who were relatively higher and lower in therapeutic conditions.[27]

Goodman's study, the first of its kind under rigorous research conditions, showed that troubled boys with companions who had high scores in openness, understanding, and warmth characteristically had higher positive psychological gains than those whose counselors had lower scores.[28]

An immense body of additional data[29] could be presented in support of our hypothesis, but in this context it is hardly necessary. For persons oriented to clinical psychology or who wish to explore further supportive research data, I would suggest Bernard Guerney's *Psychotherapeutic Agents: New Roles for Nonprofessionals, Parents and Teachers*,[30] Truax and Carkhuff's *Toward Effective Counseling and Psychotherapy: Training and Practice*, and Goodman's book just cited as the best sources.

I have proceeded in the discussion so far without specific reference to "God language" or the religious tradition. Yet I cannot leave it without three concluding comments.

1. Much of the substance of the preceding analysis of intimacy is inconspicuously under the guiding influence of the language and reflective style of Judeo-Christian interpersonalism, which I will later explore. For example, the understanding of the finitude of man, the relation of freedom and commitment, the mystery of interpersonal discovery, and much more stands in debt to the western religious tradition: the eighth-century prophets, the Talmud, the New Testament, Augustine, early monasticism, Aquinas, the Protestant tradition from Luther to Kierkegaard, and many figures of the Renaissance.

The one concept central to the Judeo-Christian tradition that deepens our perceptions of intimacy is that of covenant fidelity. Human closeness accordingly may be perceived under the analogy of the divine-human covenant, viz., God's participation in an intimate relation with the people of Israel, and through Israel, with the whole of human history. In Judeo-Christian thought, person-to-person covenant faithfulness is perceived under the illumination of the faithfulness of God toward his covenant people.

2. Yet a certain hazard occurs when we take contemporary language (however dependent upon traditional religious images) and try to translate it back into once living but now disused categories such as justification, sanctification, sin, grace, redemption, and providence. The deeper intention of the traditional categories is not always served by such a translation. Persons enamoured with novelty and modernity per se may discount nuances that are shown to have historic precedents. So up to this point I have tried to exercise a certain restraint in appealing to tradition, even though I deeply respect it, and in subsequent chapters will be addressing it directly.

3. Finally, the deepest stratum of the concept of intimacy is touched, I believe, in the idea of interpersonal communion, literally a union in which two persons *commune*, are at one together, and at one with the ground of their togetherness. Persons attain their fullest self-experience precisely within the context of their being *with* another in full presence and responsible love. Very early in the English language the word communion took on the nuance of spiritual intercourse, a form of dialogue that penetrates to certain spiritual depths. When persons encounter each other at these depths, they commune with the mystery of being that lies prior to, beyond, and within their personal meeting.[31]

A mystery is something hidden from objective analysis, although one knows it intensely through intuitive reasoning.[32] When we experience the mystery of the other person, we experience an interpersonal truth, one that is inaccessible or not fully accessible to objectivizing intelligence, yet one that is nonetheless known and apprehensible. It is not against reason, but it transcends the objective intelligence while touching it deeply. We experience the relationship as *mysterium*, an enigma not fully analyzable, a secret currently in the process of being disclosed.

This dimension leads me to prefer the term "interpersonal communion" rather than flatter behaviorist terms like "social interaction" or "dyadic interdependence" or "interpersonal complementarity." For when we point to the depths of the interpersonal life, we must grapple for frail words that hopefully will be able to point beyond themselves.

Thus we experience a certain linguistic awkwardness with phrases like I-thou, being-with-another, real presence, and interpersonal communion. For as we shall see, when persons commune, they share not only their own persons with each other, but the grounding of their own personhood in the inner meaning of reality itself.[33]

II. THE GAME−FREE RELATIONSHIP

At this point the trajectory of my argument shifts from intimacy to transactional analysis, from the intensive personal relationship to a particular way of understanding personal relationships, from the one-to-one relationship to a therapeutic strategy for dealing with the interpersonal sphere as a whole. Since my subject is not limited to intimacy, but rather intends to address more generally the dynamics of the interpersonal sphere, the next step is to broaden our perspective by looking carefully at one particular system of analysis, in fact the one now most popularly available, as a means of understanding interpersonal transactions, namely, transactional analysis (TA).

In doing so I do not cease to pursue the meaning of the game-free relationship (the transactional analyst's word for intimacy),[1] but will be asking more broadly about how transactional analysis understands the interpersonal transaction, of which intimacy is the most intensive and satisfying form, and how these understandings are rooted in the western religious tradition.

Transactional analysis is a strategy for moving persons toward intimacy. It views intimacy as the authentic end of personal meeting and the ultimately satisfying form of stroking.[2] It deserves our special attention because of its widespread use, its accessible lay vocabulary, its usefulness to nonmedically trained persons, and its hidden affinities with the western religious tradition.

Part Two performs the dual function of introducing the reader to the inner core of TA, which we will call the "implicit faith" of TA, and it will move a step beyond that to a critical dialogue with the assumptions and operational style of TA.

Some of my readers will doubtless place themselves either inside or outside the TA circle, some on the basis of sufficient, others on the basis of insufficient, knowledge. I hope to address all these people—ranging from the TA devotee to those who have had only a minimal exposure to TA, negative or positive —by introducing our discussion of TA in such a way that it is not simply a repetition of elementary TA,[3] but in effect a response to it, and yet a response that illuminates its essential features. My response to TA will be stated in such a form that even the neophyte who has not dealt with it can nonetheless come to terms with its essential form and direction.

4. Transactional Analysis: Its Implicit Faith

There is already a sizable body of literature on transactional analysis by such people as Eric Berne, Thomas Harris, Muriel James and Dorothy Jongeward, Claude Steiner, and Ira Tanner. Transactional analysis is a system developed by Eric Berne and his followers to analyze what happens between persons in encounter. The personal transaction is analyzed in terms of three ego states:

Parent	memory banks of behaviors, attitudes, gestures transmitted from parents
Adult	information-gathering capacity that orients one toward reality
Child	a repertoire of feelings shaped by early responses to parents' voices

In any interaction, one or more of these ego states is activated, so that the analysis of a transaction involves the analysis of which ego state is present or flowing in a specific interaction.[1]

Transactional analysis is unquestionably the therapeutic approach that has deluged religious communities with the widest effect in the last decade. All around the country in mostly Protestant (but some Catholic and Jewish) communities we find religious groups meeting eagerly to learn transactional analysis, and to put to work in their personal interactions the Parent, Adult, and Child concepts. Pastors are training as transactional analysts, preaching sermons that sparkle with the "inside" language of transactional analysis, and counseling with TA assumptions.[2] We find small TA groups meeting in religious settings to analyze their games, ego-states, scripts and rackets, and to trigger script releases.

Why the tremendous surge of influence of transactional analysis? And why especially in religious groups of both conservative and liberal inclinations? Since Eric Berne's *Games People Play*, two books in particular —Thomas Harris' *I'm OK—You're OK*, and James and Jongeward's *Born to Win*—have received enormously wide reading among religious groups, many of them led by religious educators. Is it possible to link transactional analysis with historical themes or echoes in these religious communities? Is TA something that has been superficially or awkwardly placed alongside the traditional religious communities and their historical experience, or is it secularized expression of something silently embedded within their historical religious experience (I will argue the latter)? Can TA be evaluated positively from the viewpoint of a tough-minded critical understanding of the Judeo-Christian tradition? Is it possible, moreover, for religious communities to transmute TA into something more profound that it now conceives of itself to be?

Many who have been involved in TA groups have had some intuition that there is a hidden kinship between their TA experience and their religious faith.[3] They may glimpse some vague similarity between God's acceptance and human acceptance, between God's forgiving OK and TA's I'm OK and you're OK. By and large, however, these intuitions have remained at a low level of generalization. Guidelines are needed now to sharpen the issues.

My basic proposal is that there is indeed an implicit theology in transactional analysis that does have a certain kinship to historical Judeo-Christian faith. If the reader resists the term "theology," I only wish that he would first understand the particular way in which I am using it. Theology is the attempt to speak consistently about the human predicament, the possibility of deliverance from that predicament, and the means of implementing that new possibility. It is clear, in this sense, that TA has implicit theological concerns, even though it may not use religious language. In order to clarify this implicit theology we must first clarify the threefold structure of all human experiencing reflected in all well-constructed theological thinking.[4]

Three questions are implicit in the lives of persons whom I have come to know well: In what sense do I understand myself to be limited and unfulfilled as a human being? What new possibilities are available that might offer me a new possibility for understanding myself anew so as to open the door for deliverance from my predicament? What ought I to do in response to these possibilities? These questions belong to the structure of human existence.

Put differently, all serious human experience is concerned with facing the limitations, conflicts, and blockages that frustrate human encounters; grasping a new vision of who we are; and searching for ways of embodying that vision, and reshaping behavior so as to implement the envisioned possibility.

This same threefold sequence implicit in all human existence is expressed explicitly in Christian worship in the triadic form of the acts of confession, thanksgiving, and commitment. Act One of the worshiping community lifts up before God the shared awareness of human inadequacy, limitation, and bondage; Act Two celebrates the new possibility for human renewal in the deliverance of God; Act Three responds to God's deliverance with an act of self-offering, in which the community commits itself to reshaping its life under the inspiration of this renewing possibility. The threefold character of worship is therefore rooted in the threefold character of the human quest.

These same three questions lie at the heart of any well-conceived theology: What is man's predicament? How has God acted to deliver humankind from that predicament? What is man's appropriate response to God's action? Therefore, worship and theology, when properly conceived, speak to issues that are embedded inevitably in human existence. In more classical language, theology reflects upon creation, redemption, and consummation. The subject of theology, consequently, is the world's need, God's action, and the awakened community's response.

Transactional analysis may be understood under this same threefold structure familiar to religious communities for many centuries. For TA deals with the human predicament, it holds out the possibility for deliverance from that predicament, and it hopes to enable a process of growth toward maturity and fulfillment in human community.

I am not merely suggesting that the transactional analysis ought to use more religious language or give lip service to religions, but rather that they are *already* functioning with an implicit theology that is amazingly thoroughgoing in character, since their work includes a detailed analysis of the bondage of the will and the plight of radical human fallenness, a therapeutic process by which persons are delivered from that bondage, and a structure and design for growth toward the good life in responsible love. It is in this sense that the views of Berne and his followers can be understood without forced interpretation in terms of this traditional threefold structure of sickness, therapy, and health (or similarly bondage, deliverance, and freedom), that embraces the perennial issues of western religious consciousness.

I will present a series of paired quotations that will show on the one hand key images of transactional analysis and on the other hand the language of the historical western religious tradition. One should not expect a precise match from each paired quotation, yet it is hoped that cumulatively they will express both similarities and differences in these two traditions. These quotations can serve as the basis of a sustained meditation on the relation between TA and Judeo-Christian language.

The Human Predicament

The first phase of the theology of Berne is his view of the human predicament, Act One of the paired quotations that follow. Elemental to all TA descriptions of the human condition are the three previously mentioned ego states: Every person has within him a set of high fidelity recordings of parent voices (colloquially called Parent tapes) that are a permanent record of an immense store of data available for instant replay. It is said that your *Parent* is in charge when you are replaying those tapes. The reality-testing process that tries to update the Parent and Child is called the *Adult*, the data-gathering function by which we learn to estimate probabilities, take in clear signals about what is happening around us, and appraise the situation objectively. The *Child* ("Kid") in me reacts in the same way as I felt when I was a little boy in the presence of my parents.

The paired quotes in Sections A (Parent, Adult, and Child) and B (Strokes and Programming) show analogies between the two languages in four different ways: (1) They show that the Parent, Adult, and Child ego states have been anticipated by Augustine's similar triadic structure of memory, understanding, and will. (2) Certain biblical narratives sharply illuminate moments when the Kid is in charge (e.g., "David danced before the Lord with all his might"), or when the Parent or Adult is in charge. (3) Paul's view of the bondage of the will, that "I can will the good but cannot do it," is very much like Berne's problem of the "decommissioned Adult," where the Adult is "reduced to an onlooker in the transaction." (4) Strokes and programming have their parallel in the religious tradition's concern for support and parental nurture.

Although the paired quotations may be used to indicate either similarities or differences between the two languages (obviously there are both), my immediate concern is to clarify some similarities, leaving it to a later section to indicate basic differences. The reader should be forewarned against the temptation of merely sampling or skimming lightly over the paired quotations, since they have a meditative intent. The full weight of the analogy will best be grasped by allowing it time to address the consciousness.

THE LANGUAGE OF TRANSACTIONAL ANALYSIS	JUDEO-CHRISTIAN LANGUAGE

ACT ONE: THE HUMAN PREDICAMENT

A. *Parent, Adult, and Child*	A. *Memory, Understanding, and Will*
When a person is in the grip of feelings, we say his child has taken over (Harris).[85]	David danced before the Lord with all his might (2 Samuel 6:14).
While one ego state has the executive power, the person may be aware of literally standing beside himself, observing his own behavior (Steiner).[6]	I do not understand my own actions. For I do not do what I want, but I do the very thing I hate (Romans 7:15).
I referred to these three parts of the personality—Parent, Adult, and Child	Since then these three, memory, understanding, will are not three lives

—as ego states. . . . These ego states determine what happens to people and what they do to and for each other. The best way, so far the neatest and most scientific way, to analyze human social and sexual relationships is to find out which ego states are involved (Berne).[7]

The Adult updates Parent data to determine what is valid and what is not, it updates Child data to determine which feelings may be expressed safely (Harris).[9]

The Adult sometimes is flooded by signals of the "bad news" variety so overwhelmingly that the Adult is reduced to an "onlooker" in the transaction. An individual in this situation might say, "I knew what I was doing was wrong, but I could not help myself" (Harris).[10]

One of the important functions of the Adult is to examine the data in the Parent, to see whether or not it is true and still applicable today, and then to accept it or reject it; and to examine the Child to see whether or not the feelings there are appropriate to the present (Harris).[11]

It might be said that the Parent is ideally suited where control is necessary. . . . The Adult is suited to situations in which accurate prediction is necessary. The Child is ideally suited where creation is desired (Steiner).[12]

but one life, nor three minds but one mind, it follows certainly that neither are they three substances but one substance . . . for not only is each contained by each, but also all by each. For I remember that I have memory, and understanding and will; and I understand that I understand, and will, and remember; and I will that I will, and remember, and understand (Augustine).[8]

When I was a child, I spoke like a child, I thought like a child, I reasoned like a child; when I became a man, I gave up childish ways (1 Corinthians 13:11).

I can will what is right, but I cannot do it. For I do not do the good I want, but the evil I do not want is what I do (Romans 7:18–19).

"You have heard that it was said, 'An eye for an eye and a tooth for a tooth.' But I say to you, Do not resist one who is evil" (Matthew 5:38–39).

We found the nature of the mind, in its memory, understanding and willing of itself, to be such that it must be apprehended as always knowing and always willing itself; and therefore also as always at the same time remembering itself. . . . These three constitute one thing, one life, one mind, one essence (Augustine).[13]

B. *Stroking and Programming*	B. *Care and Nurture*
A person needs stroking "lest his spinal cord shrivel up" (Steiner).[14]	Your honoring them will serve to encourage them and bring forth their best abilities (The Bratzlaver Rabbi).[15]
Whoever provides stroking is OK (Harris).[16]	I have calmed and quieted my soul, like a child quieted at its mother's breast; like a child that is quieted is my soul (Psalm 131:1–3).
Most programming is negative (Berne).[17]	Thou shalt not . . . (Exodus 20:13).
Recollection evoked from the temporal cortex retains the detailed character of the original experience (Penfield).[18]	In it [memory] all things are kept distinct and classified. They are carried in, each by its own channel. . . . All these the great recess of memory, and its indescribably hidden and mysterious chasms, take in, to be called to mind and reviewed, when need arises. All these things go in, each by its own gateway, and are there stored away (Augustine).[20]
The Brain functions as a high-fidelity tape recorder. . . . I not only remember how I felt. I feel the same way now (Harris).[19]	
The subject feels again the emotion which the situation originally produced in him, and he is aware of the same interpretations, true and false, which he himself gave to the experience in the first place (Penfield).[21]	Train up a child in the way he should go, and when he is old, he will not depart from it (Proverbs 22:6).

Admittedly the quotations on the right side are drawn from a wide range of constantly mutating varieties of the western religious traditions. There is no claim implied that this column comprises a cohesive statement of correct religious doctrine or orthodoxy. The reader nonetheless will recognize that even amid its diversities the Judeo-Christian tradition has substantial historical continuity and a shared language. It is that shared language which I wish to juxtapose with transactional analysis to see how they resonate in similarities and differences.

In the next sections, C (The Not-OK Position) and D (The Script Apparatus), the dynamics of the human predicament are intensified. If we think of TA as a part of the highly optimistic "human potential movement," it may be jolting to come squarely to terms with its gloomy description of the limitations of man and the melancholic dynamics of what religious traditions have called sin. For in its intergenerational concepts of the "positions" and "scripts" that we get locked into as children, TA has demythologized and restated the ancient notion of original sin. The script apparatus tyrannizes current decisions so that we are not free to will the good. There is even a restatement of the classical notion of the bondage of the will, or *yetzer ha-ra* (evil inclination), in the rabbinic tradition. The grave specter of the human quandary is seen in the fact that individuals become scripted in such a way that they do not even recognize their script. The person makes his own tracks exceptionally difficult to follow in the attempt to uncover his script apparatus. Scripts are deceiving in the special sense that the individual does not even recognize his own self-deception! Therefore, much of the effort of script and game analysis is designed to penetrate the multiple layers of defense that persons have built around their rackets so as to prevent them from recognizing the full dimensions of their predicament. All this is reminiscent of the dynamics of deception in the classical religious understanding of the radical fallenness of "Adam" ("Jeder" in TA jargon).

If sin (*hamartia* in the Greek) means missing the mark of one's true intention, then script and game analysis constitutes a fresh restatement of the dynamics of sin. (It is for good reason, however, that TA has avoided a term such as sin, which in the last century has become so abused that it now lends itself to a moralistic dilution of the human problem.)

The purpose of the paired quotations in Sections C and D, thus, is fourfold: to show that (1) the not-OK position is a frequent theme of biblical character portrayal; (2) the Hebraic tradition brilliantly grasped the *intergenerational* character of scripting, repeatedly insisting that human alienation is transmitted through the generations in perverse and ubiquitous ways; (3) many rackets and script indicators may be readily illustrated by biblical figures and events; and that (4) in all these scripty figures, both contemporary and historical, there is a certain element of comedy.

C. The Not-OK Position	C. Guilt
Very early in life every child concludes, "I'm not OK" (Harris).[22]	All who see me mock at me, they make mouths at me, they wag their heads (Psalm 22:7).
Everyone has a NOT OK child (Harris).[23]	Behold, I was brought forth in iniquity, and in sin did my mother conceive me (Psalm 51:5).
Once a position is taken, the person seeks to keep his world predictable by reinforcing it. It becomes a life position from which games are played and scripts acted out. . . . This process can be diagrammed as follows: Experiences➡Decisions➡Psychological Positions➡Script Reinforcing Behavior (James and Jongeward).[24]	By your hard and impenitent heart you are storing up wrath for yourself on the day of wrath (Romans 2:5).
"I'll kill myself because it's a lousy world where I'm no good and neither is anyone else, my friends are not much better than my enemies." In position language this reads "I'm not-OK, You're not-OK, They're not-OK" (Berne).[25]	Elijah . . . went a day's journey into the wilderness, and came and sat down under a broom tree; and he asked that he might die, saying, "It is enough; now, O Lord, take away my life; for I am no better than my fathers" (1 Kings 19:4).
D. The Script Apparatus	D. Bondage of the Will
Script: A life plan based on a decision made in childhood, reinforced by the parents, justified by subsequent events, and culminating in chosen alternative (Berne).[26]	"Behold, everyone who uses proverbs will use this proverb about you, 'like mother, like daughter.' You are the daughter of your mother, who loathed her husband and her children; and you are the sister of your sisters, who loathed their husbands and their children" (Ezekiel 16:44–45).

Each person decides in early childhood how he will live and how he will die, and that plan, which he carries in his head wherever he goes, is called his script. . . . It may not be what he wants, but it is what he wants it to be (Berne).[27]

Within his chemical limitations, whatever they are, each man has enormous possibilities for determining his own fate. Usually, however, his parents decide it for him long before he can see what they are doing (Berne).[28]

The history of human scripts can be found on ancient monuments, in courtrooms and morgues, in gambling houses and letters to the editor, and in political debates, where whole nations are taken down the righteous road by somebody trying to prove that what his parents told him in the nursery will work for the whole world (Berne).[29]

If the mother's script calls for her to be a spouseless invalid in her declining years, then one of the children must be raised from birth to stay and care for her, while the others must be taught to wander off and fill the role of ingrates (Berne).[31]

Gallows Transaction: A transaction which leads directly toward the script payoff (Berne).[33]

There are also near misses, nonwinners whose scripts require them to

"They do not know how to do right," says the Lord (Amos 3:10).

"The fathers have eaten sour grapes, and the children's teeth are set on edge" (Jeremiah 31:29)

From a putrefied root . . . have sprung putrid branches, which have transmitted their putrescence to remoter ramifications. For the children were so vitiated in their parent that they became contagious to their descendents: there was in Adam such a spring of corruption, that it is transfused from parents to children in a perpetual stream (Calvin).[30]

It is well known that children, according to the ordinary course of things, bear not only the appearance but also the moral and mental characteristiics of their parents (Luther).[32]

Judas, one of the twelve . . . drew near to Jesus to kiss him; but Jesus said to him, "Judas, would you betray the Son of Man with a kiss?" (Luke 22:47–48).

The father said to his servants, "Bring quickly the best robe. . . ." Now his work very hard, not for the purpose of winning, but just to stay even. There are "at leasters," people who say "Well, at least I didn't . . ." (Berne).[34]

elder son was in the fields (Luke 15:-22–25).

The human predicament is finally grasped in its depth, according to Berne, in its analysis of the Demonic (Section E) and Games (F). It is not incidental, I believe, that Berne has selected an overtly religious image—the demonic—to communicate the deepest stratum of the individual's bondage to scripts. The purpose of the paired quotations in E and F is (1) to point to the element of mystery in biblical images of temptation as compared with TA images of the demonic and games; (2) to show the seductive and deceitful aspect of demonic imagery in both language frames; (3) to show in both traditions the overwhelming difficulty of battling successfully the demonic inclination of the will so as actually to offer a viable possibility for health; and (4) to show that the con, the hook, and stratagems of specific games are shot through with traditional biblical images of the demonic, yet without denying human responsibility.

E. *The Demonic*

E. *The Demonic*

"Go ahead and do it!" . . . This is Daemon, the sudden supernatural push that determines a man's fate, a voice from the Golden Age, lower than the gods but higher than humanity, perhaps a fallen angel (Berne).[35]

The demons . . . struggle to have you as their slaves (Justin Martyr).[36]

Demon: (a) Urges and impulses in the child which apparently fight the script apparatus, but in reality often reinforce it. (b) The whispering voice of the Parent urging the Child on to nonadaptive impulsive behavior. The two usually coincide in their aims (Berne).[37]

Let no one say when he is tempted, "I am tempted by God," for God cannot be tempted with evil and he himself tempts no one; but each person is tempted when he is lured and enticed by his own desire (James 1:13–14).

The demon represents the most ar-

Behold, I was brought forth in

chaic layer of the personality (the Child in the child), and is there from the beginning (Berne).[38]

Daemon . . . speaks not in a loud command . . . but in a seductive whisper . . . "Come do it. Go ahead. Why not? What have you to lose but everything?" (Berne).[39]

Father's Parent on top says "Save your money," and his Child on the bottom says "Put it all on the last roll" (Berne).[40]

The come on is the Parent's voice whispering to the Child at the critical moment . . . "Come on, baby. What've you got to lose?" This is the demon in the Parent, and the demon in the Child responds. Then the Parent does a quick switch, and Jeder falls flat on his face. "There you go again," says the gleeful Parent, and Jeder answers "Ha ha!" with what is colloquially called "a shit-eating smile" (Berne).[42]

No matter how well Jeder lays his plans, the demon can come in at the critical moment and upset them all, usually with a smile and a ha ha. At the point when the therapist thinks he has four aces, Jeder plays his joker, and his demon wins the pot (Berne).[44]

F. *Games and Seduction*

Come on: A provocation or seduction into nonadaptive behavior (Berne).[46]

All games involve a con (Berne).[48]

iniquity, and in sin did my mother conceive me (Psalm 51:5).

But the serpant said to the woman, "You will not die" (Genesis 3:4).

When a little hole is opened to the devil, through which, it seems to you, he can hardly pass with his head, he has all he needs and slithers in with his entire body (Luther).[41]

The devil takes no holiday; he never rests. . . . If he cannot enter in front, he steals in at the rear. . . . He uses great cunning and many a plan. When one miscarries, he has another at hand (Luther).[43]

They [the impenitent] are like men who have contracted some disease in the private parts of the body, who conceal this from the knowledge of the physicians and thus preserve their modesty but lose their lives (Tertullian).[45]

F. *Temptation*

The devil is never straight (Luther).[47]

Again, the devil took him to a very

A con only works if there is a weakness it can hook into, a handle or "gimmick" to get hold of in the respondent, such as fear, greed, sentimentality, or irritability (Berne).[49]

Every game . . . is basically dishonest, and the outcome has a dramatic, as distinct from merely exciting, quality (Berne).[50]

A game is an ongoing series of complementary ulterior transactions progressing to a well-defined, predictable outcome. Descriptively it is a recurring set of transactions, often repetitious, superficially plausible, with a concealed motivation; or, more colloquially, a series of moves with a snare, or "gimmick" (Berne).[51]

A game provides strokes for the player, without the threat of intimacy (Steiner).[52]

. . . "sex" becomes the instrument of gamy behavior (Berne).[53]

Trading stamps, or enduring, nongenuine feelings such as anger, depres-

high mountain, and showed him all the kingdoms of the world and the glory of them; and he said to him, "All these I will give you, if you will fall down and worship me (Matthew 4:-8–9).

But the serpent said to the woman, " . . . when you eat of it your eyes will be like God, knowing good and evil" (Genesis 3:4–5).

They shouted, "Crucify, crucify him!" (Luke 23:21).

As he passed by, he saw a man blind from his birth. And his disciples asked him, "Rabbi, who sinned, this man or his parents, that he was born blind?" (John 9:1–2).

You shall eat, but not be satisfied, and there shall be hunger in your inward parts (Micah 6:14).

After a time his master's wife cast her eyes upon Joseph, and said, "Lie with me." But he refused . . . when she saw that he had left his garment in her hand . . . she called to the men of her household and said them, "See he has brought among us a Hebrew to insult us" (Genesis 39:7–14)

The Besht related the following parable: "A man asked permission of the sion, low self-esteem, sadness, etc., are "collected" and saved up by persons who play games so that when enough are accumulated they can be traded for a "free" blow-up, drunken binge, suicide attempt, or some other script milestone (Steiner).[54]

house-owner to dwell in his house. When this was refused he asked permission to hammer a nail into the wall. This request being granted, the man hammered the nail in one place, removed it, declaring the place unsuitable. Then he nailed into place after place until finally he had spoiled the entire wall. The Evil Desire behaves in a similar fashion (The Baal Shem Tov).[55]

Sometimes a person acts like a loser to win his game. For example, in a game of *Kick Me* a player provokes someone else to put him down (James and Jongeward).[56]

A wife's quarreling is a continual dripping of rain (Proverbs 19:13).

Games prevent honest, intimate, and open relationships between the players. Yet people play them because they fill up time, provoke attention, reinforce early opinions about self and others, and fulfill a sense of destiny (James and Jongeward).[57]

Man has not only been ensnared by the inferior appetites, but abominable impiety has seized the very citadel of his mind, and pride has penetrated into the inmost recesses of his heart (Calvin).[58]

Deliverance

The next part of our paired quotation meditation deals with the deliverance of persons from their human predicament. TA's understanding of the deliverance of persons from demonic powers (scripts and games) has strong echoes of the scriptural themes of exodus and deliverance. In both cases a saving new possibility is offered to persons, in the sense that their *salus* (wholeness or health) is offered as a possibility on the basis of a new understanding of their situation.

The delivering event in TA is not merely the diagnostic capacity or skill of the therapist. Rather, it is essentially expressed in an act of *permission*, which ironically is in some ways understandable as a secularized, demythologized appropriation of the biblical word of God's forgiving grace.

The therapist or group communicates to the individual permission to rewrite his script, to change his rigid adherence to repressive internal voices, and to become a more autonomous person.[59] Christian worship can celebrate with TA this permission, since it too has been grasped by a permission, a freedom to be in spite of bondage, a liberation to love in the light of our being loved by the ground and source of our being. Just as in TA groups, so in Christian community, there is celebration of dying to an old self-understanding and being born to a new one. It is in the midst of a new environment of interpersonal trust, mutual accountability, and radical permission that both communities of discourse announce a word of deliverance.[60]

But how does it happen that out of the desperate plight we have described (characterized as it is by the demonic power of scripts and games) new life emerges in freedom, accountability, love, and closeness to others? The transactional analysts have set for themselves a difficult problem since they have rightly grasped human alienation as complex and deeply enmeshed in the human condition.

For Berne the delivering event occurs essentially when a credible permission is given, either through a group member or a therapist who offers to the individual the possibility of saying no to the "curses which are laid on him by his parents."[61] At the moment that the individual grasps not only that he can become an autonomous person, but also that he will receive support from the therapeutic group in his quest for self-direction, he is on the road to script release.

There is a sense in which the mediator of this deliverance engages in a kind of descent into hell, the hell of the scripts, curses, demons, and rackets of the individual. This image is reminiscent of the Christian understanding of the incarnate participation of God in human estrangement. The mediator may be regarded as an intruder at times and his task may be difficult, but in the long run if he is to perform his mediation he must take the risk of that entry into hell and the announcement of cosmic permission, with the hope that the demonic powers will be broken.[62] Thus at the center of Berne's implicit theology stands a secularized soteriology (or understanding of salvation)[63] that offers the possibility of new life.

It is important to note, however, that the delivering event that the analyst hopes to mediate is not merely an idea. It is hardly that the therapist or group communicates to the individual the bare *idea* that he is permitted a new life-possibility. Rather it is only through the mediation of an actual *relationship through which that permission becomes credible*. That is a much more profound view of deliverance than it would be if we were just discussing the idea of permission. It is in fact more akin to, though still not identical with, the deliverance celebrated in the eucharist, which remembers God entering history in body language, not just verbalizing, as the basis of the good news.

Furthermore, the saving event is not merely mediated through professional therapists, but through a companionate *laos*, a laity, through groups of persons who share a similar hope for liberation from manipulative games. Some transactional analysts have even developed what they call permission groups, in which persons can test out new re-Parenting possibilities and, in effect, grant others permission.[64]

It may be objected that Berne's view of the delivering event is something quite different from the delivering action of God since there is no God-language or God-concept present in Berne. I agree. While pointing out the similarities, it is not my intention to equate the transactional image of deliverance with the biblical image of God's deliverance, even though they may be analogous.[65] My purpose is merely to show by means of the paired quotations where the analogies *and* differences lie, while making sure to allow TA to speak in its own vocabulary, leaving the starkest differences to be discussed later.

The purpose of the paired quotations, in Act Two on deliverance, is: (1) to show the difficulty of moving the individual from script bondage to the new life of autonomy, and how that is similar to the difficulty of repentance, in the biblical witness; (2) to show the difficulty that the therapist or group has even in bringing the individual to a rudimentary recognition of his new possibility; (3) to show in both languages the decisive function of permission so that freedom from the curse of the parental demand or law can be grasped by the person in bondage to script behavior; and (4) to show that the classical relation between law and gospel is similar to prohibition and permission in TA.

Under the conditions of sin the individual does not do what (according to his Adult) he wants to do, bound as he is by his script injunctions. But under the conditions of grace, the individual learns to live "under the Spirit," to use the language of the New Testament, instead of "under the law." He experiences a sense of Other-granted permission to live beyond his guilt and to be who he is. Although the gospel of grace and Christian freedom is easily distorted into license, or in some cases irresponsible quietism, it still is at the heart of Christian consciousness of redemption. So there remains a similarity, despite all other dissimilarities, between the grace of God that permits us to be who we are and that calls us to self-determination under this permission, and the permission of the transactional therapist who addresses the script laden with the possibility of taking charge of his own existence.

ACT TWO: DELIVERANCE

A. *The Burning of Trading Stamps*

It is just as hard for a patient to give up life long collection of hard-earned psychological trading stamps as it would be for a housewife to burn her commercial ones (Berne).[66]

In order for the patient to get better, his illusions, upon which his whole life is based, must be undermined (Berne).[68]

This is the most painful task which the script analyst has to perform: to tell his patients finally that that there is no Santa Claus. But by careful preparation, the blow can be softened and the patient may, in the long run, forgive him (Berne).[69]

In order to be cured, the patient must not only stop playing games compulsively, but must also forego the pleasure of using the stamps he has collected previously (Berne).[71]

Some people learn that psychological trading stamps are not really free, and that the collected feelings have to be paid for in loneliness, insomnia, raised

A. *The Difficulty of Repentance*

Rabbi Bunam was asked: "How can a man know if his repentance is genuine?" "If he loses the desire to commit these very offenses again," answered the Rabbi (Hasidic tradition).[67]

Enter by the narrow gate, for the gate is wide and the way is easy that leads to destruction. . . . For the gate is narrow and the way is hard that leads to life (Matthew 7:13–14).

Be wise in your reproof, lest you do more harm than good. Include yourself in any reproof. . . . Reproof that is heeded draws in its train clemency and kindness (The Bratzlaver Rabbi).[70]

It is much harder to break off one's evil habits than to split rocks. (Hasidic tradition).[72]

Nevertheless, remedies which are unpleasant justify the pain they give by the cure they effect, and they render present suffering agreeable because of blood pressure, or stomach trouble, so they stop collecting them (Berne).[73]

B. *Permission*

Permissions are the chief therapeutic instrument of the script analyst because they offer the only chance for an outsider to free the patient from the curses laid on him by his parents (Berne).[75]

In order to change or give up the script the patient needs permission to cancel these injunctions, permission not to drink, not to kill himself, so that later he may make his own autonomous choices based upon his Adult's evaluation of the real world (Crossman).[76]

Permission . . . involves giving the patient permission to do something he wishes to do, but which is in direct opposition to his Parent's wishes (Steiner).[77]

In the orthodox TA group sessions, patients can receive permission to reevaluate script-injunctions and prescriptions for getting to know the expressive Child (*Transactional Analysis Bulletin*).[78]

In the case of a 17-year-old girl with a script that demanded that she become pregnant and drop out of school as an adaptation to the injunction (Don't outdo me), permission was given "not to get pregnant and to outdo mother" through a strong, supportive, parental statement from the therapist. . . . Almost immediately, joyful relief followed. . . . The patient developed a

the advantage which is to come in the future (Tertullian).[74]

B. *Grace*

Now it is evident that no man is justified before God by the law. . . . Christ redeemed us from the curse of the law (Galatians 3:11–13).

Now before faith came, we were confined under the law, kept under restraint until faith should be revealed. So that the law was our custodian until Christ came, that we might be justified by faith. But now that faith has come, we are no longer under a custodian (Galatians 3:23–25)

For freedom Christ has set us free; stand fast therefore, and do not submit again to a yoke of slavery (Galatians 5:1).

Be good lawgivers to each other, remain faithful counsellors of each other, remove from yourselves all hypocrisy (Epistle of Barnabas).[79]

Grace has five effects in us: first, our soul is healed, second, we will good; third, we work effectively for it; fourth, we persevere; fifth, we break through to glory (St. Thomas Aquinas).[81]

Christ redeemed us from the curse of the law, having become a curse for us (Galatians 3:13).

course of life to replace the abandoned
script (Steiner).[80]

C. Script Release

Note that it was useless to say to him
"If you keep on this way you'll have a
coronary." (1) He was well aware of
that threat, and telling him again
only made him feel more miserable
because (2) he wanted a coronary,
which would free him one way or another. What he needed was not a
threat, nor an order (he already had
enough orders in his head), but a license that would liberate him from
those orders (Berne).[82]

Prohibitions hamper adaptation to
circumstances (nonadaptive), while
permissions give a free choice
(Berne).[83]

His father gave him the spellbreaker:
"You can relax if you have a coronary, ha ha." What his treatment did
was get into that part of his brain or
mind whence all these voices sent
their directives. The injunction was
then lifted by giving him permission:
"You can relax without having a
coronary" (Berne).[84]

Transactional analysis takes the superficially surprising view that an alcoholic needs permission not to
drink, because he is under duress to
do so (Steiner).[86]

Decontamination of the Adult is
. . . accomplished through an accurately timed confrontation by the
therapist's Adult (Steiner).[87]

C. Freedom

Now we are discharged from the law,
dead to that which held us captive, so
that we serve not under the old written code but in the new life of the
Spirit (Romans 7:6).

For sin will have no dominion over
you, since you are not under law but
under grace (Romans 6:12).

Sin cannot entirely take away from
man the fact that he is a rational being, for then he would no longer be
capable of sin (St. Thomas Aquinas).[85]

Live as free men, yet without using
your freedom as a pretext for evil (1
Peter 2:16).

Even if our conscience condemns us,
God is greater than our conscience. (1
John 3:20).

The New Life

The final phase of our paired quotation meditation deals with the actual reshaping of one's life-style in the light of the new possibility. How does the delivering event become an event for me?

The TA group is not merely concerned with pointing out the general possibility of freedom, but also with finding promising structures through which the individual can nurture that freedom into living embodiment. In theological language we are talking about growth in grace toward the life of responsible love in community. TA would speak of decision and intimacy with therapeutic group support. In both cases the supportive community asks the question: How does the person actually lay hold of the saving possibility so it is manifested in his daily existence? TA groups work hard on this, hoping to provide mutual support for this growth process, just as religious communities try to nurture *koinonia* and mutual pastoral care.

Just as it is the case that the goal of religious experience is the changed life, and ultimately the life of sharing the love that God shares with us, so similarly (yet differently) the goal of the TA process is an authentic life of openness to others, personal accountability, sensitivity to others, all of which is summed up in the code-word "intimacy." If in traditional theology the goal of justification is sanctification, i.e., the making whole of man and the fulfillment of the human purpose, the goal of TA is intimacy, which is a game-free relationship of openness and caring affection.

The paired quotations in Act Three on "The New Life" are intended to show that (1) the language of death and renewal that is so characteristic of Jewish apocalyptic and Christian images of conversion is also a decisive image in the TA group process; (2) in both traditions, there is an emphasis upon the freedom to become new persons despite the recalcitrant power of sin; (3) in both cases radical change or conversion involves the wager of faith and the risk of undertaking a decisive new life option; (4) much of what is encompassed in the concept of intimacy is a secularized way of "speaking the truth in love" of which the New Testament speaks; (5) the biblical image of sexuality centering on the concept of two persons becoming one flesh (*henosis*) resonates deeply with the TA concept of intimacy; (6) intimacy is not to be understood in merely a sexual or erotic sense, but in both traditions in a mystical sense as being in touch with the unifying center of reality.

ACT THREE: THE NEW LIFE

A. *Decision*

Mort turned in his cancer card and resumed his membership in the human race (Berne).[88]

We do not drift into a new position. It is a decision we make. In this respect it is like a conversion experience (Harris).[89]

The object of script analysis is to "close the show and put a better one on the road" (Berne).[90]

Ursula Steiner . . . demonstrated some of the exercises and activities which are used (for Permission Classes) . . . culminating in a spectacularly loud and active singing and dancing accompaniment to the record "Ding, Dong, the Witch is Dead" (Claude and Ursula Steiner).[92]

"Since yesterday I feel grown up, and I feel that I have come alive" (patient quoted by David Kupfer).[94]

Although the early experiences which culminated in the position cannot be erased, I believe the early position can be changed. What was once decided can be undecided (Harris).[95]

A. *Conversion*

The dead shall arise and praise thee (Psalm 88).

Behold, I make all things new (Revelation 21:5).

"Who is the penitent man"? Rabbi Judah said: "The man who, when the same opportunity for sin occurs once or twice, refrains from sinning" (Rabbi Judah ben Ezekiel).[91]

My sins are blotted out, and I, even I, am reconciled to God (John Wesley).[93]

It was fitting to make merry and be glad, for this your brother was dead, and is alive (Luke 15:32).

Why should not human nature be raised to a higher state after sin than might otherwise have been the case? God permits evil in order to bring forth a greater good. St. Paul says, where sin abounded, grace did more abound (St. Thomas Aquinas).[96]

Like diseases, scripts have an onset, a course, and an outcome. Because of this similarity, scripts have been mistaken for diseases. However because scripts are based on consciously willed decisions rather than on morbid tissue changes, they can be revoked or "undecided" by similarly willed decisions (Steiner).[97]

The remedy against demons . . . Every loser should carry it in wallet or purse, and whenever success looms in sight, that is the moment of danger. Then when the demon whispers "Stretch out your arm—and put the whole wad on one last number, or have just one drink, or now is the time to pull your knife, or grab her (him) by the neck" . . . or whatever the losing movement is, pull the arm back and say it loud and clear: "But mother, I'd rather do it my own way and win" (Berne).[99]

The first three positions [I'M NOT OK—YOU'RE OK, I'M NOT OK—YOU'RE NOT OK, I'M OK—YOU'RE NOT OK] are based on feelings. The fourth is based on thought, faith, and the wager of action (Harris).[101]

B. *Intimacy*

Beyond games lies . . . intimacy . . . a candid game-free relationship, with mutual free giving and receiving and without exploitation (Berne).[103]

Some people prefer to talk straight rather than play games: that is, they

If the human race does not have the power by free choice to avoid what is shameful and to choose what is right, then there is no responsibility for actions of any kind (Justin Martyr).[98]

Christ says that the devil is the prince of this world . . . and a liar. If, then, we would and must live upon earth, we must realize that we are guests and lodge in an inn with a knave as host and with an inscription or a sign over the door which reads *The House of Murder* or *The House of Lies.* . . . That is the devil's trade and his work; that is the way he keeps house; that is how business is carried on in this inn . . . whoever is his guest must expect and risk experiencing rough treatment (Luther).[100]

How will you wager? . . . You have two things to lose: the true and the good; and two things to stake: your reason and your will, your knowledge and your happiness; and your nature has two things to avoid: error and wretchedness (Pascal).[102]

B. *The Mystery of Love*

Love covers a multitude of sins (1 Peter 4:8).

When the Lord himself was asked by someone when his kingdom would will not act provocatively in order to get trading stamps, and will refuse to respond to the spurious provocative behavior of others. With the energy thus saved, they are ready when they meet the right person at the right time in the right place for more legitimate expressions of feeling (Berne).[104]

When people get to know each other well, they penetrate through the script into the depths where this real Self resides. . . . Sex . . . replaces after-burn and reach-back with warm-up and afterglow (Berne).[106]

Recovering the capacity for intimacy is a major goal of TA (James and Jongeward).[107]

Be willing to happen to somebody, and somebody will happen to you (Berne).[108]

Intimacy: A person at a concert briefly catches the eye of a stranger. For that moment they are aware of the bond of mutual enjoyment. They smile openly at each other in a moment of intimacy. A husband and wife at work weeding their garden experience a sense of closeness which spontaneously leads to physical contact that validates their affections (James and Jongeward).[110]

C. Wholeness

. . . love . . . is nature's psychotherapy (Berne).[112]

come, he said: "When the two shall be one, and the outside as the inside, and the male with the female neither male nor female." Now "the two are one" when we speak with one another in truth, and there is but one soul in two bodies without dissimulation (Second Epistle of Clement).[105]

Therefore a man leaves his father and his mother and cleaves to his wife, and they become one flesh. And the man and his wife were both naked, and were not ashamed (Genesis 2:24–25).

Beloved, let us love one another; for love is of God, and he who loves is born of God and knows God (1 John 4:7).

If I am not for myself who will be? And if I am only for myself, what am I? And if not now, when? (Rabbi Hillel).[109]

This is the mystery of the oneness of God, that at whatever place I, a tiny bit, lay hold of it, I lay hold of the whole (The Baal Shem Tov).[111]

C. Fulfillment

There is no fear in love, but perfect love casts out fear. For fear has to do

Intimacy involves genuine caring (James and Jongeward).[113]

The converse of the script is the real person living in a real world (Berne).[115]

Some preaching should be Parent (stroking) and some Adult (teaching), but clergymen need to recognize that the highest form of living is Child to Child and that the purpose of worship is to enable people to be intimate (Everts).[116]

What do you say after you say Hello? This childlike question, so apparently artless and free of the profundity expected of scientific inquiry, really contains within itself all the basic questions of human living and all the fundamental problems of the social sciences (Berne).[118]

To say Hello rightly is to see the other person, to be aware of him as a phenomenon, to happen to him and to be ready for him to happen to you (Berne).[119]

with punishment, and he who fears is not perfected in love (1 John 4:18)

Our feast explains itself by its name. The Greeks call it love (Tertullian).[114]

"But a Samaritan, as he journeyed, came to where he was; and when he saw him, he had compassion, and went to him and bound up his wounds . . . and brought him to an inn" (Luke 10:33–34).

There are false affections, and there are true. A man's having much affection, don't prove that he has any true religion: but if he has no affection, it proves he has no true religion (Jonathan Edwards).[117]

He who loves his neighbor has fulfilled the law (Romans 13:8).

Another Zaddik once cried from the depth of his heart: "Would I could love the best of men as tenderly as God loves the worst" (Rabbi Schmelke).[120]

Leaving criticisms of TA to a subsequent chapter, I have tried to show how transactional analysis expresses an implicit theology that unconsciously is parallel to the Judeo-Christian understanding of the human quandary, the saving possibility and the life of love.

5. A Letter to Frogs and Princes

Normally I find the life of a professor pleasantly predictable. I can always count on a knock on my door approximately twenty minutes after examination papers have been returned. I always know that February will be the longest month of the year. And I can always be certain that book orders marked "urgent" will arrive weeks late.

As is my habit every autumn, I offer one course on a contemporary theme, another on some historical problem. Last fall these two classes had quite different projects: one was studying transactional analysis, while the other was deep into Paul's letter to Rome. It so happened that midway through the semester I had some work to submit from both courses to the stenographic pool, one office in the university that always functions efficiently. I needed a transcription of a videotape of a group doing transactional analysis, and some retyped lecture notes on the theology of Paul's Romans. Confidently I put these two typing tasks in the campus mail on Monday, knowing that by Thursday the ever-faithful service would have them back to me in the usual four days.

The following Thursday morning I went to pick up my mail. There was the packet from the steno service, felicitously packaged in its usual brown manila folder with a neatly looped string. Judiciously, I opened it for inspection. There it was with perfect margins, typed as usual in executive format, with a sharp imprint and a perfect carbon. Casually

I glanced across the first page. It was then that I began to experience a vague sense of uneasiness. Now with full concentration I started again at the top of the page. By the middle of the page I decided I had better sit down.

For what I had submitted as two separate manuscripts had gotten inseparably scrambled. I stared in disbelief.

I am still pondering the dilemma of whether I should try to sort out the two manuscripts or to send it back to the stenographic pool and let them unscramble it.

Yet as I read further, despite the fact that the outcome was far different than I had intended, I have decided to include it in this section, leaving it to the reader to sort it out himself.[1]

Fragments From a Letter of Paul to the Transactional Analysts

I

[1]This letter comes to you from Paul to clarify the You're OK of God which has been long ago anticipated by wise men in ancient scriptures.

[2]The OK of God is centered in the story of a particular man [3]born in the lineage of David, [4] who by a mighty act of God rose from the dead. [5]It is through meeting him personally that I have received the privilege of a commission [6] to address on his behalf all frogs and princes, all the script-laden, and all whose sweatshirts read "Kick me."

[7]I send greetings to all of you in Frisco, and to permission groups everywhere. [8]Let me begin by giving thanks for all of you. [9]For all over the world they are talking about what you have done, and the script releases which you have gotten hold of (or which have gotten hold of you). [10]God knows how continually I have hoped that somehow I might succeed in communicating with you significantly. [11]I would sincerely like to be there with you, to bring you some spiritual gift, or to put it more accurately, [12]I would like to be among you to receive encouragement myself through the influence of your faith on me as of mine on you. [13]For I have a hunch that you especially will welcome the word of God's OK just as so many others around the world are celebrating it.

[14]I find myself equally challenged by both secularists and religionists. This good news deserves to be clarified to everybody, rich and poor, gifted and deprived, winners and losers. [15]So I am eager to come among

your groups to talk about the decisive therapeutic event in human history. [16]For I am not ashamed of God's OK. [17]It is God's own spell-breaker for everyone who is able to receive it wholeheartedly—not just for religious folk but in a larger sense everyone—because here we finally come to know God's way of turning persons around. It begins and ends in candor and trust. For as the scripture says: "Those who really live, live in terms of radical trust in the One who gives us life."

[18]The place to begin is with what you call script analysis, but I would like to broaden it to include not just individual scripts but the whole of history. People's lives are messed up, shipwrecked all about us. The structures of life for many are falling apart. Because of their security operations, people must hide the truth about themselves. They have to protect themselves against awareness of what they know most deeply about themselves.

[19]The truth about things is plain before our eyes, everyone's eyes. If we only let our Adult take charge in looking at things, the truth will be apparent. To the eyes of reason, the reality of things is made known. [20]So people are not so convincing when they offer elaborate excuses about how they did not let their Adult understanding guide them to reality.

[21]The result is that people grope ever more deeply in darkness. The momentum of their thinking has increasingly become "I'm not OK / You're not OK / They're not OK." [22]Even though they may seem to have wisdom, they are really making fools of themselves, [23]because they are pretending that relative goods are absolute.

[24]For this reason, the God who gives them freedom originally lets them go ahead and live in a hell of their own making. God in effect says that if they must insist on wasting the valuable gift of life, then they will pay the price of having missed life. It is so sad to see this human waste. [25]Look around you and see how persons have forfeited their true existence, and accepted a phony lie about themselves.

[26]Just look at what has resulted. The best clue to human distortions may be seen in interpersonal distortions. The best clue to interpersonal alienation is to look at the twisted character of sexuality in our time. Many are not even allowing their own sexuality to emerge in natural heterosexual ways. [27]Men turn away from natural sexual intercourse with women. Intimacy is reduced to a pornographic image of lustful grabbing

and manipulative ploys. Of course when this happens, the consequences of these distortions have their own impact on human personalities.

[28]Again the ultimate Giver of human freedom permits persons in desperate pursuit of their own imagined freedom to become enslaved, if they insist, to their own degeneracy. So they find themselves more and more deeply caught in scripted positions. Their life becomes a prison.

[29]Look at the Earthian population. It is not hard to find people who are rotten, greedy and malicious. They feel so not-OK themselves that they become steeped in envy, quarrelsomeness and spite. They have an endless repertoire of gimmicks. Their actions are covert. [30]They stab people in the back. They are arrogant and boastful. In third-degree tissue games the result is suicide and murder. [31]Their minds team with diabolical invention, trying to hook others into their stamp-collecting rackets. They con. They do not listen to their Adult speaking. Many have lost the capacity for intimacy.

[32]There is a level at which people involved in this scene already know their own damnation. Yet incredibly they not only continue to make a hell for themselves, but also try to hook others into collusive behaviors.

II

[1]Now, if you think I have been talking about these people as if you and I are better than they, or that we can set ourselves up as judges of them, then let me make it clear that none of us is in a position to do so. [2]For whenever we begin condemning others, the result is that we condemn ourselves. [3]For everybody is involved in these games. So we should not put each other down. [4]For what makes you think you can so accurately judge the deceptive behaviors of others while considering yourself so game-free? [5]Maybe you transactional analysts who are so quick to point to others' games may be storing up for yourselves [6]a big switch in the last days when everything will be appropriately judged. [7]If you patiently do good and try to mediate a healing influence in the world rather than trying to put people down, then that is far better . . .

III

⁹Do not think that just because you know the language of psychology and psychotherapy that you are so far out ahead of others. All persons fall short of what they know to be to the good of their neighbor and even their own self-interest. ¹⁰The scriptures have said this long before: "No one lives without playing games. No one is really straight, No, not one. ¹¹No one really understands. No one seeks the truth. ¹²All have turned aside. . . ." ¹⁹So if we measure ourselves by what our best moral knowledge tells us is right, we have to conclude that the straight edge of the absolute moral demand shows us all how crooked we are. ²⁰The radical claim of our conscience to do the good shows us all how inadequate we are before it.

²¹This is just the point at which God's OK comes into the picture. For we are now seeing that the OK of God has been declared, even in spite of our radical failures to live up to Parent expectations. ²²This is God's way of putting persons back on their feet again and letting them take charge of their own existence. For anyone who really trusts in the OKing event of God, for which the shorthand term is Jesus Christ, God's OK becomes effective in him, regardless of who he is.

²³For everyone has fallen short of the moral demands to which he knows himself accountable, internalized in his Parent tapes. ²⁴All have fallen short—²⁵now all are OK before the One who gives us life. ²⁶It is as if the slate had been wiped clean.

²⁷So what happens to all of our desperate efforts to make others think we are OK? There is really no need to struggle to be OK anymore. You are now free to see things on a different plane, that of God's OK rather than merely your own struggle for OKness. ²⁸When you respond by putting your trust in God's own spellbreaker, it is no longer necessary for you to struggle to achieve your OKness by trying endlessly to fulfill parental injunctions. . . .

³¹Does this mean that we are undermining the Parent? Does this amount to an attack on all moral consciousness, simply because we trust in God's OK? By no means. Rather we are now viewing the moral consciousness in its proper place. We are putting the law on a firmer footing. . . .

V

¹Now that we have been set up on our feet through putting our trust in the OK of God, it is important for us to grasp the fact that we now *have* peace. *Shalom!* We have already received God's verdict which was expected only at the end of history. The verdict came through an event whose code name is Jesus Christ. ²We have been invited to stand up confidently in the presence of the One who gives us life. Because Jesus was raised from the dead, this gives us a strong confidence in what is in store for us in the future.

³That does not mean we are pointed only toward the future. It is possible for us to be joyful now, even in the midst of our hassles with ourselves and others. ⁴Even the difficulties we experience with others train us to hang in there. ⁵When we do, we are never really disappointed. As we look toward the end in history, that makes us all the more able to struggle with the hassles of this sphere.

⁶Get this: When we were helplessly mired in our scripts, Jesus the Messiah came to die on a cross for every lousy one of us. ⁷You can hardly find anyone ready to die even for good people, even though that sometimes happens. ⁸But what we have here is a good man who died for us precisely while we were all messed up, not while we were good or had finally fulfilled our scripts, but precisely amid our compulsiveness and ego-distortions. ⁹That is when God's word of OK came to us. ¹⁰Now I ask you, if God OKed us amid our phoniness and self-assertiveness, what do we have to fear? ¹¹What it amounts to is that while we were rejecting the life that the Giver of life gives us, he was out dying for us trying to restore us to our true selves. This is the ground upon which our community is certain that history is in a new phase.

¹²Think about the whole course of history with me. Let us imagine that all of our human destinies were mythically bound up in one person. In your writings you have called him Jeder, meaning Everyman. ¹³Let us suppose that this whole complex intergenerational process of human scripting and distortion were all wrapped up in Jeder, this one Earthian. ¹⁴The history of Jeder is the history of death. ¹⁵Once the human race began to get locked into scripts and episcripts, no one has seemed to be

able to break free from it because he himself was caught in the scripting process.

¹⁶But Jeder's existence anticipates its fulfillment in another figure who is to come—the expected Messiah. ¹⁷If the old history is wrapped up in Jeder, a new history has begun in this new man, Christ, who embodies God's OK to humanity. ¹⁸Under Jeder, everyone had been stuck with a big stroke-deficit. With the coming of God's OK, everyone gets a new start with a bundle of strokes from God himself. ¹⁹So persons are set on their feet again. This is not just for a few but for all persons. . . .

VI

¹So what should our response be? Should we just wallow in the new liberty which is given us by God's OK, just because we now have room to? Shall we see how far we can exploit the generosity of God? ²Certainly not. ³For do you not understand that when Jesus was buried, you were buried with him? ⁴And just as the good, eternally nurturing Father raised Jesus from the dead, so you too have been raised into new life.

⁵So don't keep on surrendering the limbs of your body to the old dead person, Jeder. ⁶Let your body be alive to the promise of a new history. ⁷If you do this there is no way you can be stuck in the old dead life-style, because you are not now living under the legitimate authority of dead Parent tapes, ⁹but in a live here-and-now relation to the neighbor in love, in response to God's own love. . . .

¹²It is as if the person you once were is now dead, crucified with Christ. ¹³We now no longer need to be slaves to our former scripts. ¹⁴ Dead men do not have to sweat out stinking scripts. You are dead men, in that sense, and alive in a greater sense.

¹⁵What comes next? Shall we just do our thing, live it up? Are we going to say we are no longer under any demands, protected by God's unconditional OK? Of course not. God is not Santa Claus. ¹⁶Do you not understand that you used to be slaves to your scripts and trips, but now it is possible to be free. You used to give your bodies to the employment of an old boss—the old, destructive Parent tapes. ¹⁷Now you can come into more fulfilling employment. ¹⁸You can take charge yourselves. ¹⁹It is as if your bodies were now employed by you yourself under the

permission of the OKing God, and you owe no further debt to your previous employer. . . .

VII

[1]You cannot be unaware, my friends (for I am speaking to you who have some knowledge of Parent tapes), that a person must deal with these Parent inputs only as long as he lives and no longer. [2]Let me give you an illustration. A married woman is bound by long-standing injunctions to stay with her husband as long as he lives, but if her husband dies she is free to marry another man without any stigma. [3]Let us suppose that you are married to a man who is going to live forever, but you are in love with someone else. The only way you can get out of your first marriage is to die yourself. [4]That is just the place where we are. We have been "married" to all sorts of dubious moral demands through which we had hoped to obtain fulfillment. [5]But our "marriage" to these legalistic demands is over when we died with Jesus. [6]Our "marriage" to Jesus began when we rose with him from the dead.

[7]What follows then? Does this mean that the Parent ego state is identical with sickness? Is not the Parent the cause of all our problems? Of course not. We would not even know what it means to be bad if it were not for parents. We would never have known the meaning of honesty if our parents had not said "You shall not bear false witness."

[8]It was just through such parenting, however, that our striving for OKness got messed up. Let us go back to the beginning. [9]There was, in fact, a time in my earliest childhood when I knew none of those parental demands. They loved me unconditionally. I was fully alive to my feelings. But when those parent demands began to press in upon my consciousness, when their strokes became conditional, I began the process of denying some of my feelings—then more and more, especially if I could only get strokes by doing so. So I began to lose touch with myself. A part of me was lost, namely that part of me that was fully in touch with my experiencing process. [10]The parental injunctions which should have led me to fulfillment proved to lead me to nonfulfillment, [11]because the Daemon in my will found an opportunity through these injunctions to seduce me into thinking that I could earn my basic OKness through strict obedience to them. [12]Therefore we can say that

the parental concerns in themselves may be good. They are intended for life. But they lead inadvertently to death.

[13]Am I then laying the blame on these Parent tapes, so that I come off smelling like a rose? That would be a cop-out. For I colluded with those parenting inputs. I am not going to portray myself as "victim." My own self-assertive inclination showed its true character by using a good thing to bring about my nonfulfillment.

[14]Here is the peculiar conflict I experience as a result: [15]I do not even acknowledge my own actions as mine. I disown parts of me which are not OK. For what I do is not what I want to do, but what I detest doing. [16]I do not seem to be fully in charge of my own existence. It is as if the parental injunctions and my collusion with them had in fact taken over. Even though my adapted Child may consent to the parental inputs, still I find my will divided. [17]The result is that I do not actually do what I myself most deeply will. As things are, it is no longer I who perform the action, but these scripted parental tapes that lodge inside my consciousness. [18]There is even a sense in which it seems that there is very little left of my own original will, striving for the good. It is as if my will were lying captive to my own collusions with parental injunctions.

Although I may have a certain intention to do the good, I cannot seem to do it.[19] For the good, toward which my Adult points me and to which I want to consent, I fail to do. Instead I do the very thing which is against my Adult. When my Adult is contaminated in this way, it is as if I have two wills which conflict: my Parent which tells me what I ought to do, and my Child which tells me what I want to do.[20] My Adult reality-orientation is caught helplessly in the middle, so much so that you might say that it is not exactly "I" who am doing what I prefer not to do, but rather it is my adapted Child colluding with the archaic Parent lodging in my consciousness. [21] Just at the point at which I know what is right, the only thing within my reach seems to be the Parental tape with which I have colluded. It is as if I am scripted to do the wrong thing, to be a loser.

[22]In my inmost self I continue to be in touch with reality, but in my bodily behavior it seems as if something else is at work, a different momentum which fights against the law of my Adult, the data of which my reason approves. [23] This, in effect makes me a prisoner, locking me into my own archaic collusions. [24] Under these conditions, I despair over

my whole existence. I cry out for deliverance from this compulsive bondage of my will which seems to be scripting me to futility and death. I hear a gallows laugh echoing out of my own scripted consciousness. What possible new avenue might be open to me?

VIII

[1]Thanks be to God, it is now possible for us to take a new direction. For God himself has triggered a script release for us all. [2]In the light of God's end-time OK to all men, it is possible for us to break free from the unyielding momentum of this deadly course.

For in the light of God's OK, we stand under a new cosmic *permission*. The Parent claims have lost their demonic power. [3]God himself has done what the parent concerns were trying to do but, due to their history of scripting, could not, namely, he has given us his own final OK. By coming to us in his own way, in a form like our own, God himself engages in our struggle, in effect takes on our nature, and in a momentous healing event renders outmoded our whole effort to overcome stroke-deficits by trying to be the perfectly adapted Child. [4]Thus we are no longer under the control of these self-defeating hamartic scripts, but now we are energized by a higher spirit. . . .

[12]Now if this spirit of God's OK dwells in you, then it follows that witch parent injunctions now have no claim upon you. You are permitted to say No to them. You are no longer indebted to them. You no longer have to give them your life and loyalty. [13]If you continue to live in their employment, you have just chosen to tune out this good news. But if you wake up to what God has done in history, then you will begin to live again. [15]The spirit we have received does not make us slaves, afraid of God, but like children who call him "Daddy." That is what Jesus meant when he addressed the Giver of life as "Abba" (Papa). It means that we now embrace God as the good nurturing Parent, not as merely a legally oppressive pig Parent. [16]The spirit whispers deep inside us that we really are kids in this Daddy's family. [17]Everything a good Father has, of course, belongs to his children too. That is why we know that everything our "Abba" has given to Jesus, he is going to give us too. . . .

XII

[1]Therefore, my companions, I invite you into a new way of life. [2]Do not let the weight of a dying history squeeze you into its mold. Instead, break its spell by letting God's OK give you a brand new outlook. Then you will be able to come alive again and enjoy the kind of life for which you are intended. . . .

[10]Let God's OK flow through you. Turn off the witch messages and stay with the Great Permission . . . [13]You are now free to practice openness, hospitality, to contribute to whomever has needs. Be there wherever your neighbor is. Share with him his real existence. [14]If somebody curses you or tries to destroy you, try to get in touch with where that person really is so you can do something good for him. [15]With the joyful be joyful. Mourn with the mourners.

[16]Do not think you have all the answers. [17]Do not pay back evil for evil. [18]Live at peace with everyone you meet. [19]If someone hooks your not-OK Kid, do not try to get even with him. For the scriptures say that God will do all the getting even. . . .

XIII

[8]Finally, keep in mind that whoever really loves those around him has satisfied every legitimate claim of the law, everything that is worthwhile in parental instruction. [9]For all the commandments like "Put sexuality in the context of sustained covenant fidelity" or "Do not rip off things that belong to others," "Do not kill anyone," and the rest are summed up essentially in one rule, "Love your neighbor as yourself." [10]For genuine love is not motivated to rip people off or break someone's trust. So the whole realm of ethics and the whole intent of parental nurture is summed up in one word: love.

6. Who Says You're OK? — A Critique of Transactional Analysis

Since transactional analysis is the most widely employed system for understanding interpersonal relationships at present, it deserves our best critical response. The purpose of these critical reflections is not to discredit TA, but to take it seriously enough to seek to amend it constructively, build upon it, develop its insights more profoundly, nurture it to greater profundity, strengthen its weaknesses, and unfold some of its hidden implications. It is by this means that I hope to take some steps, as previously promised, "beyond transactional analysis."

The Ontology of OK-ness

Upon what basis does TA therapy so confidently affirm your OKness or my OKness? Who says we're so OK?

Although popularized by Thomas Harris, the language of the OK positions was earlier developed by Eric Berne and others in the early sixties.[1] There are, according to Berne, "four basic positions from which games and scripts are played, and which program the person so that he has something to say after he says Hello":

I'm not OK / You're OK (the depressive position)
I'm OK / You're not OK (the paranoid position)
I'm not OK / You're not OK (the schizoid position)
I'm OK / You're OK (the healthy position)[2]

Berne further divides the positions into the following "three-handed positions":

I'm OK / You're OK / They're OK (the ideal position)
I'm OK / You're OK / They're not OK (snob position of gang or demagogue)
I'm OK / You're not OK / They're OK (agitator, missionary, and malcontent)
I'm OK / You're not OK / They're not OK (arrogant, self-righteous critic)
I'm not OK / You're OK / They're OK (self-punishing masochist)
I'm not OK / You're OK / They're not OK (servile, self-abasement)
I'm not OK / You're not OK / They're OK (servile envy)
I'm not OK / You're not OK / They're not OK (pessimistic futility)[3]

In all the descriptions the OK position is preferred as the sound, wholesome, and successful one. I'm OK / You're OK is, according to Berne, "the 'healthy' position (or in treatment, the get-well one), the best one for decent living." It is the "get on with" position, the "winner's" position.[4]

The OK position is the most reality-oriented. There seems to be something inherently *right* about it. It is "intrinsically constructive."[5] It is in tune with the *reality* of things. Thus it becomes an ontological statement, a statement about being, about the way things *are*. When we are most in touch with the real situation in which we exist, we affirm ourselves and others. I suggest that there is therefore a tacit ontological assumption (an assumption about the nature of being) in transactional analysis, that *it is not merely other persons who do the OKing, but something in reality itself.* Let me explain.

All therapeutic processes have ontological assumptions, i.e., they assume something about being itself, or the nature of reality. Any time we concern ourselves with personality growth, we make assumptions about the good and the real (ethics and ontology). We define health in terms of that which is most reality-oriented, and thus most in touch with actual being itself.

When we learn through script-release to say to each other I'm OK and you're OK, this occurs not just on the narrow assumption that you are privately acceptable to me as a person but on the much more profound assumption that you are in fact OK as a human being. Your OKness does not depend strictly upon my granting it to you. When you see yourself appropriately in the light of reality you know you are OK. So I am not the source of acceptance, finally, although I may point to an acceptance that has its source beyond me. You are not ultimately the source of my acceptance, but rather you may point to an acceptance that has its source beyond our mutual accepting or rejecting. The assumption is, moreover, that you are acceptable despite the fact that I may momentarily *reject* you, and that I am OK even when you are rejecting me![6]

As evidence for this assumption, we need only look at the way which a TA group deals with the script-laden individual. It tries to communicate to the person that there is nothing in *reality itself* (which the Adult data-gathering process examines) that fates him to script behavior. As a result, TA processes assume that persons *ought not* to be scripted, game-tyrannized or intimacy-deprived. It is an offence against their humanity for persons to spend their lives conning others, not talking straight, and never knowing closeness.[7]

Transactional analysts are clearly aware of the fact that there are plausible reasons why persons get locked into games, rackets, and scripts, but the presence of these self-destructive behaviors does not change the way things are or stand as a fundamental redefinition of being. In fact, TA theories refuse to admit that there is in reality any substantial ground for legitimating the not-OK positions or for scripted behavior. For they are trying to deliver the individual from a scripted not-OK position to a "reality orientation."

There are much more profound philosophical assumptions than are ordinarily recognized in the TA literature, but they are nonetheless operational assumptions. This is an implicit philosophy that is put to work in relationships, even though it may remain unrecognized by its exponents.

Now I move from ontology to theology. Having established this ontological assumption, we are only a short step from scriptural affirmations. For Judeo-Christian theology speaks explicitly of that which the therapeutic process only implicitly assumes. The implicit understanding that we are in reality fundamentally OK is an explicit concern of Judeo-Christian worship.

The ground of our OKness reveals himself in history, according to the biblical witness. God lets us know through historical events that we are, despite our sins, OK, affirmed, accepted, embraced with infinite forgiving love. Jews and Christians celebrate God's affirmation of Israel and finally of the whole of humanity, not merely as an idea in our heads but as an event in history.[8]

However important it may be for persons to be able to say I'm OK, that says very little about the source of OKness. Judeo-Christian memory has a lot to say about the source of history's OKness. For if that ground of our hope has not really met us in history, but is merely an idea in our heads, then how are we to trust in it? That is what the biblical good news is all about: the ground of our acceptance has in fact met us in history!

Thus the purpose of preaching is to call persons to an awareness of the reality of the situation in which they already exist, the reality of God's OKing love; not to introduce God to the self as if He were not already there, but to introduce the person to himself as one who has already been claimed and affirmed by the source of all things.

Christian worship celebrates the entry into history of the Word, which clarifies once for all that we are in fact OK in the presence of the One who gives us life. The liturgy celebrates the ground of our *being* OK, not merely *feeling* OK.

I am not implying that the term OK adequately carries the full weight of the Judeo-Christian understanding of the infinite love of God. God's self-sacrificial agape is always something more than saying "you're OK." To be forgiven by God is something more than feeling OK.

OK means acceptable. Love means far more than "acceptable." One does not read a letter from one's beloved in the same way that one reads a letter from one who accepts him. The infinite love of God is infinitely more than human feelings of acceptance.

Accordingly, it is significant that Harris's book was not entitled *I'm Forgiven—You're Forgiven*. OKness is hardly as profound as the holy self-giving love manifested on the cross. When God announces to history, "You are forgiven," He does it in a radical nonverbal body-language statement of cross and resurrection.[9] The point is that the OK image is flat in comparison to the New Testament images of God's approach to humanity. I do not wish to protest the OK image, but rather to note that it can be illuminated by analogy to God's forgiving love.

All such explicit theology is of course completely absent in Berne and his followers. They simply address a humanistic OK without inquiring into its ontological (much less theological) assumptions. Christian theology has little to be jealous of and nothing to be disturbed about in the secularized, humanistic OK. But it joyfully beholds that humanistic affirmation from within the context of its perception of God's affirmation of history, which enables more deeply our own self-affirmation and the affirmation of our neighbor.

Let us not forget that in the western religious tradition we also learn to say "you're *not* OK, and neither am I." Rejecting behaviors are hardly to be ruled out of Judeo-Christian consciousness. Read the Bible. Christ said "No, you are not OK," to the moneychangers he drove out of the temple. Nathan said "No, you are far from OK," to David's murderous lechery. "You are not OK," said Amos and Jeremiah repeatedly to Israel.[10]

The worshiping community teaches us how better to say "God, I am not OK," without self-debasement. That is what confession is all about. We stand before God and acknowledge that our behavior is unacceptable in terms of the covenant commitments we have made (Psalms 32 and 51). In terms of the values we hold dear, we have failed to be responsible both to our neighbors and to the One who gives us life. Yet it is precisely in the midst of the most serious awareness of our inadequacy that the word of forgiveness is addressed. Self-acceptance is therefore based upon the awareness not that we have fully met our covenantal responsibilities, but that grace works mysteriously through our inadequacies to redeem our alienated relationships.[11]

Games Transactional Analysts Play

Having given TA a sympathetic hearing, it is now appropriate to examine our hesitations about it. Where are its excesses, unexamined weaknesses, and inner inconsistencies? How may the dialogue now be advanced on the basis of a clear-headed grasp of these differences?

Despite its evident usefulness, there is a fair amount in TA about which we may reasonably be disturbed: its steady put-down of the Parent, its romanticism, some of its skewed value assumptions, its underlying hedonism, its in-group language, and a fairly heavy bag of other thorny issues. I will pursue these issues by focusing principally on the works of Eric Berne, rather than dealing in detail with TA popularizers such as Thomas Harris and Muriel James, since the essential problems of the system, I believe, come directly from its founder.

THE PIG PARENT

Although Berne denies that he is being unkind to parents, the logic of his language and the force of his rhetoric lands almost without exception on the side of children against parents. Always the parenting voice is the witch, devil, ogre, or pig.[12]

At a time when actual parents and children are having tough times communicating on the same wavelength,[13] TA comes on with what to many seems to be a steady put-down of the necessary constraining parent inputs into the formation of consciousness.

Unfortunately the polemic is not merely against parents, but tends to diffuse and expand almost infinitely so as to stand against tradition, against historical continuity, against social cohesion and all the mechanisms of social constraint.[14] Religious and moral reflection at its best has valued those mechanisms, even while pointing to their relativity and tendency to become idolatrous or legalistic.

Quite rightly Berne distinguishes between the prejudicial Parent (who sets up prohibitive nonrational injunctions) and the nurturing Parent (who offers wise support and sympathy).[15] In the heat of rhetoric, however, that crucial distinction gets lost. What does come through clearly is passionate talk about release from the bondage of repressive Parent tapes.

Similarly he distinguishes between the adapted Child, who is adapted to parental influence, and the natural Child, who expresses native energies spontaneously.[16] Again the rhetorical force lands on the side of the natural Child as good, resourceful, and needing release, and the adapted Child as usually dysfunctional, constricted, immobilized, dehumanizing, and something to be escaped from.

For Berne it is "the adaptation to parental influences"[17] that spoils the natural child. I ask how a child could mature without parental constraint?

TA may inadvertently increase the problems of communication between children and parents by leading children to believe that their basic scripts and problems are dumped on them by their parents without their own collusion. This can easily become an invitation to disown the very responsibility that TA elsewhere wishes to encourage.[18]

I myself am much more attracted to an earlier statement by psychiatrist Edmund Bergler in *Parents Not Guilty of Their Children's' Neuroses*.[19] An increasing number of parents suffer unrealistic and misplaced guilt over their children's presumed neurotic behavior. Unintentionally the TA rhetoric intensifies that guilt. It offers me the tempting opportunity to blame my parents for my scripty behaviors and irresponsibilities.

Is the Bible all that mistaken when it calls persons to "Honor your father and your mother, that your days may be long in the land which the Lord your God gives you."[20] In traditional Judeo-Christian ethics, the honoring of father and mother is the center of a whole system of social cohesiveness through which a society holds together and functions organically. If parental credibility is lost, the result tends to be disastrous for all of the other structures of society: education, the state, the economy, and so forth.

Frankly, I doubt that our society needs freedom from parental injunctions more than intergenerational reconciliation. Our deepest predicament, according to Berne, is that we are locked too rigidly into script-determining Parent voices. The opposite hypothesis needs to be entertained seriously. What if our most critical problems were rather that we have no means of implementing parental injunctions, and therefore social continuity?[21] As a parent, I am inclined to see this as my hairiest task, for which I get little help from Berne. The deeper problem may be that we do not know how to use our freedom responsibly, rather than that we do not have enough freedom.[22]

I do not see the overbearing patriarchal father as the central identity problem of contemporary persons. Far from it. The father is too often either evasive, weak, or not even there.

To deepen the dilemma further, Berne so emphasizes the formative influence of the first five years that he tends to underestimate the influence of peer groups as substitute Parent tapes in the adolescent period. His argument tends to support adolescents in their struggle against parental tyranny, but fails to see the tyrannical temptations of peer-group parenting that are so decisive in our culture at certain age levels.

In fact, TA may best be understood as an adolescent psychotherapy. All of the values that adolescents struggle for—autonomy, self-direction against parent voices, ego strength against the superego — are central to TA. One could almost fantasize that all Berne's clients were adolescents. It may be that he has spoken relevantly to the part of society that is struggling deeply with adolescent-like questions, but other social values such as continuity and discipline are neglected.[23]

AFTER INTIMACY, WHAT?

There are six ways people can structure their time in order to get strokes, according to Berne: withdrawal, ritual, activities (or work), pastimes, games, and intimacy.[24] When two or more persons are *not* withdrawing, meeting ritualistically, working, or playing games or at pastimes, then they are experiencing intimacy. If you put people in a room and find ways to eliminate their opportunities to withdraw, to trade ritual strokes, engage in activities, pastimes, and games, he says, the result will be intimacy. Withdrawal, ritual, pastimes, and games are inadequate ways of satisfying stroke hunger, and in fact constitute the main obstacles to the real point of human living, which is intimacy.[25]

Without any derogation of the need for intimacy, it may be high time to reaffirm the sociological function of withdrawal, work, ritual behaviors, pastimes, and games. All are necessary for interpersonal health.

Intimacy is not the only objective in interpersonal relationships. In fact, if there were no rituals or activities or work or operational patterns to accomplish tasks, then it would be difficult even to imagine sustaining a social context in which to search for intimacy. Hobbes and Hegel rightly knew that a reliable and orderly social context is necessary in order for the more intimate interpersonal gifts to be exchanged and personal values pursued.

The exceptionally high value place upon intimacy and the corresponding rejection of other modes of structuring time is a peculiarly class-oriented value assumption. The urgent, almost frenetic, quest for intimacy is endemic to upper-middle-class, white-collar, competitive, upwardly socially mobile Americans who are in fact the principal clientele of psychotherapy, whose cultural assumptions fit Berne's value assumptions hand in glove. It is their values (upward mobility, autonomy, winning, achieving, receiving strokes, individualistic freedom, etc.) to which Berne's therapy corresponds and appeals. In my opinion these values are most understandable in the light of the particular recent history of that particular class, and cannot reasonably be generalized to describe the human condition.

Ask yourself how a poor Kentucky coal miner or a black musician or a South Dakota wheat farmer's wife or an underground poet in San Diego or almost anyone from the Third World would fit into the typical TA group and you have the problem in a nutshell. Psychotherapy and group processes in general have been notoriously irrelevant to the values of class strata other than the one from which their basic clientele is drawn.

TA is not alone among psychotherapies in assuming that its values are universally applicable to all men in all times, yet even the most cursory sociological criticism of current psychotherapy indicates that therapeutic value systems orbit around the assumed values of a specific social class. It is a part of the general myopia of TA, and psychotherapy in general, that it neglects any sociological assessment of its implicitly assumed values.[26] These criticisms doubtless are telling ones when put to a system that assumes its values are universally shared by all reasonable beings.

It should not be forgotten also that TA is a polemical literature as well as therapy. It not only stands for a value system, but it implicitly (and sometimes explicitly) stands against alternative values. The value system against which TA is most decisively struggling, surprisingly, is precisely the so-called Protestant ethic that spawned many of the religious communities it is now servicing.[27] The Protestant work ethic orbits around the this-worldly asceticism that values hard work and productiveness, is strongly oriented toward structures of social cooperation and relatively less toward individual freedom. Ironically, TA has attacked that value system in its home court at a time when it is vulnerable. Oddly enough, however, TA may be in other ways as thoroughly bourgeois as the bourgeois values it appears to protest, since it appeals essentially to a clientele of small property owners and social managers and controllers who trade professionally on high degrees of personal self-confidence.

After persons have achieved intimacy, what comes next? Nothing much of importance (as the TA literature often seems to assume) or something of even greater value? The religious communities have always known that a great deal comes after our personal subjective stroking. After intimacy we must still learn to be accountable to our neighbors within the structures of human community. After intimacy we still must maintain the continuity of our social structures, families, and political processes.

Even more broadly, the rest of history is yet to be accomplished beyond our personal intimacies. When TA so concentrates on interpersonal, subjective values that it loses sight of the historical and cosmic process, its constricted vision loses credibility. However important, intimacy must be placed within a historical context that comprises many other values, some of which challenge intimacy and all of which stand within the larger context of the ground and giver of all values.

A more circumspect understanding of reality will see the interpersonal within the context of the social, and social in the context of the historical, and the historical as inclusive not only of its past and present, but of its future and finally its end. So when you and I meet, we meet in the midst of a history that reaches far beyond our interpersonal meeting.

THE TEMPTATIONS OF JARGON

"Transactional analysis in the space of ten years," according to Berne, "has evolved its own complete indigenous culture, with its own traditions, etiquette, character, contracts and artifacts."[28] Although Berne says there must be "no cultishness or exclusiveness" in the TA subculture, the momentum clearly seems to be in that direction. This tendency becomes most evident in the pop in-group jargon that the local inhabitants of that subculture have developed and that continues to proliferate.

I sympathize with the desire of TA to develop a colloquial language, but sometimes it becomes a bit peculiar. In one uncommonly awful paragraph entitled "Bags and Things," for instance, Berne writes: "A person who breaks out of a bag (or 'container,' as it is sometimes called) will immediately proceed to do his thing. . . ."[29] Meaning what? In the attempt to flow with the stream of pop culture, language may become so diluted that it does not refer to anything at all.

When Berne confidently concludes that "the object of script analysis is to turn frogs into princes,"[30] we have not merely an overstated caricature of the task of therapy, but more a fundamental oversimplification of the human predicament. Although this comic tendency to exaggerate is part of TA's attractiveness, it leads the careful observer to a certain distrust of facile categories.

Similarly, Berne proposes that "there are two kinds of people in the world: real people and plastic people. . . . The real people make their own decisions, while the plastic people are run by fortune cookies."[31] These colloquial exaggerations are all topped, however, by a sober announcement in the *Transactional Analysis Bulletin* reporting "permission classes" at an Indiana hospital under one Jim Jones, who says he intends to "hook the Adults of the patients to look at and turn off the witch messages that clobber the freed up natural Child"![32]

This inveterate tendency to oversimplify is best seen in the so-called sweatshirt mottos, whose function is to indicate on the front who you are and how you want people to expect you to come on. On the back is the "kicker," which indicates what they are actually going to get out of your transaction. Among classical sweatshirt mottos are, for example, the Sisyphus script, the front of which says, "I'm a super salesman"; the back says, "But don't buy anything from me." (Sisyphus is a loser's script, since every time he gets near the top of the hill, he has to start all over again. When he approaches his goal he must then find some reason not to get there.) An alcoholic script may have on the front: "I'm

Proud I'm an Alcoholic," with the kicker, "But Remember It's a Sickness." A transexual script—sweatshirt front: "Don't You Think I'm Fascinating?" The back: "Isn't That Enough?" Then there is the "old soldiers never die" script, which says on the front, "I'm a Nice Guy," while on the back it says, "Even If It Kills Me."[33] However amusing these may be, they illustrate the strong momentum in TA toward colloquial oversimplification and comic caricature and to the one-liner put-down, which easily become facile and hardly reassuring.

Not merely the inconsequential colloquialisms, however, but the central images used by Berne often seem arbitrary; for example, his definition of games: A game must have a con, which "hooks into a gimmick, so that the respondent responds," plus a "switch" followed by a "crossup," "after which both players collect their payoffs. . . . Whatever fits this formula is a game, and whatever does not fit it is not a game."[34] The definition is more self-limiting than Berne's own descriptions of games allow. It requires too many disclaimers to make it useful. To those who think of games as one of the most healthy, enjoyable things people do, the coopting of the term game for interpersonal deception is unfortunate and a bit unfair.[35]

As a whole, the TA vocabulary tends to speak in comic caricatures that often have the nuance of a put-down, and that do not build exceptional confidence in the reader that the system is really interested in understanding the inner dynamics of the pig Parent or the frog son or the fairy godmother. The clowning language would be more defensible if it were not so consistently linked with harsh and relentless polemics.

THE WIN-LOSE MOTIF

Since Berne introduced the notion of the loser (frog) and winner (prince) into therapeutic practice, it has been taken over heartily by most of the TA writers: Harris, Steiner, and especially James and Jongeward, who conspicuously titled their books *Born to Win* and *Winning with People.*[36]

The win-lose motif carries with it all the problems of the American competitive ideas of success and failure. Despite disclaimers, it imposes an ill-chosen image of acquisitiveness upon the process of personal growth that it could happily do without. It cashes in on and exploits the

American success ideal by linking it with therapeutic change. Far from being identified as one, the two should be sharply distinguished.

In addition to these objections, a more profound understanding of suffering will reveal that losing is often a means to growth. Among psychologists, Viktor Frankl shows that living within limits may deepen one's sense of personal freedom.[37] That confounds the winner-loser dichotomy.

Great lives in the religious tradition have often been viewed as losers. Kierkegaard lost his beloved, his intended vocation, his health, many of his friends, his public respect, and his livelihood. He was by wide consensus a loser. Yet many are still addressed profoundly by his works. Socrates was a loser. He lost his family, his reputation, and finally his life because of his teaching, and yet he is held to be the father of philosophy. Jesus Christ may be the prototypical loser. Yet it is only through his "losing" that the meaning of his life is expressed to us, precisely through the cross, precisely through rejection. The resurrection is the final confounding of the loser image.

The moral depth of TA hardly ever extends beyond simple hedonism. Actions are valued in terms of their ability to maximize pleasure and minimize suffering. The religious tradition questions that assumption radically. Suffering may be constructive. It may test one's moral courage. The thorn in the flesh may become a means of grace, teaching us of our finitude and instructing us in faith and hope.[38]

THE POSITIVE FUNCTION OF GUILT

The work of O. H. Mowrer,[39] a distinguished behavioral psychologist and former president of the American Psychological Association, presents an interesting contrast and challenge to Berne's views. Neurotic behavior, according to Mowrer, results precisely from one's failure to live up to the moral demands that he has internalized. Mowrer thinks that the guilt we feel is "real guilt" in the presence of actual negated values, whereas for Berne the guilt is not rooted in reality and therapy becomes deliverance from that guilt. Berne wants to provide a permission to be released from these internalized demands. Mowrer's opposite view focuses on confession of guilt, or what he calls "publishing one's sins," coupled with serious acts of restitution to restore broken covenants. His basic model for a lay therapy is Alcoholics Anonymous, wherein one not only confesses one's failures openly, but also engages in specific acts of restitution for anyone against whom he has done wrong. Berne speaks neither of confession nor restitution.

According to Mowrer, the real problem in so-called mental disorder is the *isolation* that results from one's being afraid to tell others of the values he has negated. TA, quite oppositely, treats the internalized moral injunctions more as part of the pathology than the cure. If Mowrer is correct, then TA intensifies the problem of guilt and isolation and makes the pathology deeper in the long run.

What Berne negatively calls Parent, Mowrer positively calls *conscience*, which when violated elicits guilt. This condition is not a sickness, but the result of specific wrongdoing and irresponsibility.[40] Oppositely, Berne seems to argue that the rejection of parentally dominated conscience is precisely the road to health. For Mowrer it is the road to misery. For after one has done what he understands to be wrong, he tries to cover up his act, and it is this secrecy that gives rise to the symptoms of pathological disorder.

What is needed, according to Mowrer, is not merely an understanding of the dynamics of games and scripts, but also positive acts of confession and restitution in the presence of relevant others, where one accounts to others for his lack of responsibility toward values that his conscience clearly tells him are obligatory or right. The only real cure to be found is in acts of actual restoration, which change the objective situation so that one no longer feels guilty and needs to hide it.

If Mowrer is correct, then TA re-Parenting may increase debilitating guilt, since it supplies group support to the ego or Adult ego state to say no to Parent-dominated "conscience" and to "moral injunctions." In fact, it is precisely the distressing fact that man is a moral being with a conscience that constitutes the essential condition from which Berne apparently wishes to find a means of escape.[41]

This is not the context in which we can solve all the differences between Berne and Mowrer, but we can at least point out that the issue between them has been a continuing dilemma in the history of religious ethics. The dialectic between *law* and *gospel*[42] (Augustine, Luther,

Calvin, Kierkegaard) is a classical religious attempt to solve the basic dilemma expressed in the multidimensional conflict between Berne and Mowrer.

THE RISKS OF RE-PARENTING

A final problem I have with transactional therapy is its notion of re-Parenting, which Berne defines as "cutting off early Parental programming and substituting a new and more adaptive program through regression. . . ."[43] There is to me a horrifying *hubris* in the assumption that therapy thoroughly reworks the early history of the troubled person. The notion that therapy has as its task the liquidation of parental inputs and the instigation of a new "superior" set of programs reminds me of Nazi attempts to abolish the old order and set up a "new" order, fresh from the drawing boards of social visionaries.

Much of what Berne calls the witch Parent and script injunctions, from which he wishes to free us, are part of an enormously complex social apparatus that manifests itself subjectively in *conscience*. Much of that apparatus would have to be laboriously reformulated if it were now exterminated by social experimentation.[44]

It may be that the religious communities will have to assert themselves again as a corrective to experimentalist exaggerations and hasty, impatient disrespect for organic human traditioning. The Judeo-Christian heritage is capable of leading us again to take seriously the recalcitrance of human self-assertiveness without losing sight of the human potentiality.

Berne speaks at times as if all social constraint were inimical to the human spirit.[45] It is precisely these constraints that are, in my opinion, often are ultimately friendly to human freedom and in fact necessary for social existence. I would not wish to live in a society that had no structure whatever, no moral tradition, no way of mediating values through parental injunctions. The alternatives to the present, albeit imperfect, system may be more horrifying than we might suppose.

From the rabbinic tradition we learn that man, inclined as he is to protect his own interest at the expense of his neighbor, makes it quite necessary for societies to create laws, limits, and structures that guarantee at least a minimal degree of justice and order.[46] It is dangerous, history has found, to rely upon the fleeting goodwill and charisma of human benevolence without any structures of coercive justice. At times it seems that Berne would thoughtlessly return us to the vulnerable condition that Hobbes called the "state of nature,"[47] where every man's hand is against every man, and life is poor, nasty, brutish, and short, since there is no legitimate power to constrain evil.

Historically Berne is explainable within the framework of the romanticist wing of American individualism, which sees human hope essentially in terms of individual freedom *from* social constraint and rational ordering. The tradition that offers the most resourceful corrective is the classical religious interpersonalism that we find in the Talmud, Augustine, Luther, Suarez, Hobbes, Newman, Burke, and in the twentieth century preeminently in Reinhold Niebuhr. It is a realistic tradition that, without ceasing to be hopeful for historical change, nonetheless values just social constraints without idolizing them.

At first blush TA appears to be a highly original theory of personality and therapy. This appearance is reinforced both by the avid faith of its true believers and by the mass movement character of TA enterprise. Upon closer inspection, however, TA is probably not as innovative as it first appears. The notion of the decommissioned Adult, for example, is a restatement of a theme deeply written into the Greek philosophical tradition and well sustained throughout medieval philosophy to enlightenment rationalism and empiricism, viz., that it is the task of the rational (data-gathering Adult) capacities to guide the self in the light of factual observation and without prejudice, without being predisposed by unexamined moral injunctions or presuppositions. Long before Berne we find the British ethical tradition from Bacon to Hume talking of the need to open one's eyes to sense data rather than to let one's rational processes be predefined prejudicially.[48] Greek philosophy similarly wanted to avoid the contamination of (Adult) rational processes either by one's libidinal energies (Child) or by unexamined preconceptions (Parent).[49] A greater historical consciousness surely would reveal that such seemingly original ideas of TA are a refurbishing of already known options in the western intellectual tradition. (Far from being a put-down, that is an attempt to honor TA historically more than it would wish to honor itself or see itself honored.)

However earnestly Berne may have believed that TA provides a "complete personality diagram of any human being whatsoever, encompassing everything he may feel, think, say, or do,"[50] I feel that TA exaggerates the profundity of its grasp of the human condition and ignores alternative models for understanding interpersonal behavior.

After such severe criticisms, one might wonder why we have ever given our attention to transactional analysis, and why religious communities find themselves even slightly enamoured by it? Isn't the distance so great as to make further dialogue hopeless?

No. There is still good reason to pursue the dialogue, despite the problems we have mentioned, for the following reasons:

1. Transactional analysis continues to be a widespread, broadly based ubiquitous lay movement both within and without religious communities aimed at the healing of human suffering, interpersonal growth, and the recovery of intimacy. These goals are shared by religious communities. However inadequate some of its theoretical models may be, nonetheless it shares this arena with religious communities as a partner in search of human wholeness.

2. As I have detailed in Chapter 4, there still remain profound parallels between the language of transactional analysis and the western religious tradition that deserve continuing exploration, meditation, and sharpening.

3. TA is commendable as a simplified, colloquial lay therapy, a populist attempt to release the therapeutic resources of ordinary people at a time when persons experience decreasing confidence in the medical-practitioner model of therapeutic change.

III. A THEOLOGY OF INTERPERSONAL COMMUNION

As my recent study *The Intensive Group Experience* showed, there is good reason to expect that the encounter culture and religious communities will have something decisive to contribute to each other. Systematic theological reflection must now work to utilize the energies spawned by the encounter culture and to harness them on behalf of Judeo-Christian thought and spiritual formation.

Is it possible to take the learnings, achievements, and interpersonal strategies of the encounter culture and build a style of theological reflection out of them? My purpose is to clarify a way of thinking about the Judeo-Christian tradition *from within* the matrix of here-and-now interpersonal transactions. I am convinced that significant theological reflection can emerge immediately, contextually, and concretely out of here-and-now personal encounters. The work of the encounter culture,[1] which is specifically concerned with facilitating and interpreting personal encounter, offers a creative laboratory matrix in which to work theologically.[2] Our task is to search for a self-consistent and deliberate theological grasp of I-thou encounter.

At least two pitfalls must be avoided: the temptation (1) to overlay on top of interpersonal experiences alien theological categories, language, and images that are not germane to the experience itself, and (2) to allow a profoundly moving peak experience or significant interpersonal meeting to remain uninterpreted and out of touch with the classical understandings of religious community and thus misplace its historical identity through lack of articulation.

7. The Task of Transactional Theology

As I survey the diffuse scene of contemporary religious thought, I am amazed and disappointed at its inveterate tendency toward individualism. It is basically an *intra*personal literature. Ponder for a moment the significant titles on the interpersonal motif in religious experience. Chances are you will not think of much between Buber and Oraison. While the individual is a frequent theme of theology, the *inter*personal is a rare theme, and where it is occasionally found it is not often treated in depth.

I became curious several years ago as to whether it might be possible to develop a sustained religious reflection out of concrete experiential contexts where interpersonal encounter is intensified. The current momentum of academic theology is decidedly resistant to thinking explicitly about particular here-and-now personal encounters. It was that momentum that disturbed me and made me wonder whether an encounter-oriented, experiential theology was possible. Furthermore I sensed, after a decade of teaching theology and ethics in the Barthian-Bultmannian-Niebuhrian tradition, that I was not really in touch with my companions, students, family, and neighbors in the direct, open, authentic way I in which I fancied myself to be. It was in this way that the need to think theologically about the interpersonal arose di-

101

rectly out of the malaise of my own interpersonal experience. It really began about six years ago when some of my more courageous students confronted me with the fact that my mode of personal meeting was hardly what I imagined it was. I discovered that there was a severe disjunction between the way I thought I dealt with others and the way others perceived themselves as being dealt with by me. Quite astonished, this started me on the path that led to *The Intensive Group Experience* and finally to this more systematic inquiry into interpersonal communion.

The Learning Matrix

Accordingly I wish now to describe a particular educational experiment that I have been involved with over the last five years, which has shaped the entire reflection that follows, and in fact much of the preceding material. Both for lay religious groups and for theological students I have conducted seminars in a "Theology of Personal Transactions," an experience-based learning process focusing on "what happens between us as persons." The learning experience moves through three distinct phases, utilizing three different educational models and formats in each of three five-week periods (using the fifteen-week semester as the normal time span), as follows.

The first phase of the learning design, "Introduction to a Theology of Personal Transactions," utilizes a lecture format with all class sessions devoted to classical theological models for understanding the interpersonal sphere. Here the participant is introduced to some basic structures of theological reflection (Kierkegaard's aesthetic, ethical, and religious stages,[1] Buber's I-Thou and I-It, Aquinas on nature and grace; Luther on law and gospel; Augustine's *caritas* synthesis,[2] etc.). Further effort is made to introduce the participant to certain structures of psychological analysis of interpersonal relationships (the Leary octants, Goffman's interaction analysis, Sullivan's interpersonal psychiatry, Berne and Steiner on transactional analysis, Schutz's FIRO construct, the Johari window and other NTL contributions, Shostrom's Gestalt view of manipulation, Thibaut and Kelley's matrix analysis, Bales's interaction process analysis, etc.).[3]

Then, having grasped some of the basic categories for reflecting theologically upon the interpersonal sphere, the design moves into a second phase that uses a laboratory learning format, with no formal agenda except the group's own interpersonal transactions. In extended time sessions (one session of four to six hours a week), we meet each other in group encounter to deal with each other's preferred behavioral styles, using a variety of intensive group strategies including T-group, Gestalt awareness training, transactional analysis (including structural, game, and script analysis) and to some degree sociometric and matrix analysis. The purpose is to meet each other, offer feedback in effective ways, and understand ourselves and what is happening between us. All sessions are videotaped. Nothing overtly theological is designed into the second phase and quite often the specifically religious language remains at a minimum.

The third phase involves a substantial shift to a seminar format in which we address ourselves deliberately to "Theologizing About Our Own Transactions." Ordinarily we receive one paper from each participant analyzing what happened between us in one videotaped laboratory session, or one segment of it, and how it can be understood theologically, employing the language and analytical perspectives of the biblical witness and the Judeo-Christian tradition. Among the categories of the theological tradition that participants have found useful in analyzing their interactions are sin, grace, forgiveness, the demonic, covenant, guilt, revelation, hope, idolatry, judgment, providence, atonement, freedom, bondage of the will, and mystery.

Such is the five-year experiment that stands behind all my own thinking about a theology of personal transactions. The many laymen and students who have participated in these groups have helped me immensely to think theologically about interpersonal meeting, and without the perceptive insights that emerged out of this process I would have very little to say. Much of what follows is thus an attempt to give some methodological clarification to the process of transactional theology in which we have for some time been engaged: to show that it can be done, how it can be done, and to ask what it implies for the future of religious communities.

When we speak of deriving theological reflections and affirmations out of a particular transaction, it is important that we not thoughtlessly tear the fabric of Christian theology so its wholeness is misplaced or lost sight of. My intent is not to derive a particular doctrine out of a particular transaction, but to move situationally into and out of the transaction with some glimpse of the wholeness of the wisdom of the Christian tradition. Christian social philosophy provides a set of understandings that one brings to the transaction, but those understandings are further illuminated and mobilized in the light of specific encounters in ways that might have been impossible without those encounters. Far from claiming or even attempting to achieve any sort of complete accounting of Christian doctrine, or a *summa* of transactional theology, I am only modestly hoping to allow theological reflection to be addressed by specific transactions, and to allow specific transactions to be addressed by theology, confident that the dialogue will be mutually beneficial to all concerned. The transactional theologian thus becomes not only a group facilitator but also a broker between the language of group encounter and the traditional language of the religious community.

The Scope of a Theology of Personal Transactions

Our task is to learn to reflect theologically (and not only psychologically) upon how persons meet and behold each other, how they induce each other to action, how their feelings toward each other flow and quietly arrange the conditions for verbal meeting and how the history of their interaction moves from one locus and tone to another, and toward what destiny.

The basic unit to be investigated is the interpersonal dyad.[4] In the interest of clarity and greater precision I focus particularly upon the one-to-one, face-to-face interaction. What happens, from the perspective of the western religious memory, when two persons meet in intimacy and understanding? Or meet in the mode of rejection, estrangement, or indifference? Or collude so as to elicit self-destructive or creative behaviors from each other? How is the meeting to be grasped in relation to God's own meeting with human history?

We take the dyad as the basic unit of social interaction, however, without denying the crucial importance and influence of larger social structures and interactive processes. It is beyond the present range of our interest to try to do justice to all of these complex influences which admittedly pour into the dyadic transaction from the families, peer groups, institutional role expectations, class stratification, of the two persons who meet in dyadic interaction. Rather, our focus necessarily will be upon the specific dynamics of one-to-one meeting, always aware, however, of the mysteries of social existence that lie beyond and shape the one-to-one encounter.

The case study method is consistent with the essential character of transactional theology, which without denying them does not begin operationally with classical structures of theology or with the a priori religious nature of man or with the triune doctrine of God, (even though it may end there), but rather emerges concretely out of persons meeting persons. The procedure is to move from transaction A to theological reflection A', from transaction B to theological reflection B', and so on, and in this way to build not a finished systematic theology but a method of doing theology based on making transparent the deeper nature of interpersonal transactions. Without any theological imperialism, or any suggestion that this way of doing theology is the only or best way, I am suggesting that personal transactions offer the religious communities an enticing and significant constellation of experiential materials for theological reflection.

I do not intend to claim that the method of transactional theology is new to the twentieth century or has no precedents in religious history. Although the preconditioning elements of this model are heavily dependent upon the current encounter culture, I have already shown[5] that these recent encounter processes have their roots deep in the western religious tradition, particularly in Protestant and Jewish pietism of the eighteenth century. A related task is to show further in a plausible way that transactional theology has significant prototypes in western religious history.

In the Hebraic tradition the prophetic word characteristically moves out of historical experience, and very often directly out of interpersonal encounter. Moses before the pharaoh, Nathan's confrontation with David, or Amos's confrontation with Amaziah, for example, displays a style of reflection on God's self-revelation in history that develops directly out of concrete interpersonal encounter. Job is another example of a mode of theologizing that emerges directly out of personal experience. The chief prototype of a theology of personal transactions is Jesus, whose messianic vocation leads him into intense interpersonal encounters, such as with the woman at the well, the man born blind, tax collectors, disciples, and authorities. He is remembered as teaching and proclaiming his message directly out of these specific encounters.[6]

Further exploration in the history of the tradition of transactional theology could involve similar patterns in Paul, Augustine, Aquinas, Luther, Kierkegaard, and others, asking in each case how personal meeting functions for theology. More recent attempts to recover an experiential-relational theology are found in the works of Buber, Tournier, Oraison, H. R. Niebuhr, and Frank Lake.[7]

In the same context, I am keenly interested in the task of spiritual formation and that of the spiritual director as they are being formulated in the light of the contributions of the encounter culture. What the psychotherapeutic and encounter styles of spiritual direction have not achieved, however, is a perspective that can be contributed by the Judeo-Christian tradition, namely, an understanding of universal history that reshapes the direction of and enriches the quality of spiritual formation.[8]

I conceive of our exercise from beginning to end as an exercise in evangelical theology. I am quite prepared to give my reader some latitude if he does not choose to use the term "evangelical" with me, but what I mean by evangelical theology is an attempt to think about life, or in this case interpersonal transactions, from within the framework of the gospel, God's good news of his own prototypical transaction with man that is decisively glimpsed in the cross and resurrection of Jesus.

The general framework in which I would like to think about interpersonal transactions is the analogy between human transactions and God's transactions with man. That may sound like an attempt at innovation, but I do not consider it so, since the Christian community has for a long time been talking about "transactional theology." For classical Christology is a model of thinking about God and man that sees as the center of history an archetypal "transaction," the code word for which is the Christ event.

I want to outline a method and style for theologizing concretely out of interpersonal experience, utilizing the intensive group experience as a laboratory for improved feedback in person-to-person encounter. In doing so, however, I do not want to slip into the position of merely *using* theological categories pragmatically or valuing theological reasoning solely on the basis of its pragmatic applicability to human change processes. If a theology of personal transactions is to be accountable to its own distinctive subject matter, viz., the self-revelation of God in history, then it must be able to address the interpersonal realm with its own integrity, and not merely acquiescently borrow insights from interpersonal psychology. It must do something more than try to produce good results interpersonally. It must address both the functional or dysfunctional personal transaction with its own understanding of history and human existence. I hope such an exercise will show the usefulness of theology without making utility the criteria by which theological statements are to be judged.

Historic Christian Personalism

St. Thomas Aquinas argued that "the good of one person is worth more than the good of the whole universe of nature."[9] It can be plausibly stated that the high valuation of the person is a gift to secularizing man from the Judeo-Christian understanding of the personal God. "The infinite value of human personality" is not an invention of Kant, but his reappropriation of a continuing tradition of Judeo-Christian personalism.

Although the quest for the meaning of the personal is hardly new to the twentieth century, it does seem that the form that the quest has taken in the twentieth century has had some distinctive features. A powerful personalist aspiration emerged in the 1920s.[10] The fact that it was perceived and expressed by such varied persons who had little or no contact with each other (Buber, Ebner, Maritain, Berdyaev, and Gogarten) indicates that something occurred in early twentieth-century European culture that enabled such an expression to flower. (Ironically, their main link may be that they were all reading Søren Kierkegaard.) The historian of ideas, however, cannot help but notice that in the 1920s the study of the interpersonal took on decisively new momentum. It was not altogether new, but it was brilliantly and poetically stated, and addressed to a cultural situation more ready to hear of *I and Thou* than any previous period.

Since the patristic period, Christian interpersonal philosophy has spoken not only of the dignity of the human person and of the claim upon persons to enter into authentic, just, open and loving communication, but also of the person's calling to participate in the shaping of the common good. Christian personalism has distinguished itself from all social philosophies that would focus primarily on the individual and his private good, his private self-actualization or pleasure. Classical Christian social philosophy beholds the person as ordained to the enjoyment and glorification of God as the person's ultimate end. In the meeting of persons we meet the source and ground of personhood. Therefore the *telos* of interpersonal relationships is not simply the private good of the individuals, or any created good finally, but rather that which transcends and enables all goods, namely, the creator of persons, the personal God.[12]

The personal transaction is not viewed by Christian social philosophy as an end in itself, but as a means to bring the person to his ultimate end, namely, sharing in the knowledge and love of God, and living in fellowship with God and others. It is often through the love of persons that the love of God is made most credible, even though the love of God is not reducible to any particular act of human loving.

Maritain perceptively views the solitude of the beatific vision and the monastic visionary as a "most inhabited solitude," because in it "another society is formed—the society of the multitude of blessed souls, each of which on its own account beholds the divine essence and enjoys the same uncreated Good. They love mutually in God."[13] This same balance of individual identity and social enjoyment is expressed classically by Augustine, who describes the peace of the celestial city as a perfectly ordered and harmonious "enjoyment of God, and of one another in God."[14]

Aquinas similarly affirmed the discipline of meditation as a means of greater, not less, sociality, if sociality is seen properly to be also fellowship with God and through God fellowship with others.[15] It may be that a contemporary theology of the interpersonal is being called anew in our time to stress the value of the meditative life precisely as a means to the renewal of the interpersonal. Admittedly, withdrawal can become a pernicious enemy of the interpersonal, but it is in the interest of the interpersonal to have the witness of the holy one, the saint, whose life of prayer points beyond the interpersonal to that which transcends and embraces all interpersonal meeting.[16]

In the last two decades, several factors in our cultural history have conspired to make necessary a restatement of the achievements of the Judeo-Christian personalism of the 1920s and 1930s.[17] Although innumerable influences have shaped this new context, there are four in particular that make the earlier literature on interpersonal theology somewhat dated and inadequate:

1. Interpersonal meeting is shaped and misshaped today by the particular range of problems that are endemic to advanced industrial civilization, particularly increasing mobility, materialistic reductionism, and depersonalization.

2. The new electronic communications environment shapes and misshapes interpersonal meeting by channeling it through electronic media that reduce face-to-face exchanges and increase enormously the possibility of long distance exchanges.

3. The encounter culture has set before us a new possibility and a new demand for candor and openness in interpersonal dealings. It can be understood as a part of the "revolution of rising expectations" in the realm of the interpersonal.

4. The behavioral sciences have accelerated sharply their empirical inquiry into the dynamics of the interpersonal, resulting in an enormous backlog of significant new data on interpersonal behavior that cries out for attention and evaluation by Judeo-Christian personalism.

Partner Disciplines in the Quest for Interpersonal Understanding

Although theology cannot begin to undertake this task without the companionship of other disciplines, it is called to make clear the distinctiveness of its own task and ground. What follows is an attempt to clarify the sense in which a theology of interpersonal communion is interdependent with other disciplines addressing themselves to the realm of the interpersonal, and yet distinguishable, although not separable, from those partner disciplines.

Since theology is certainly not the only discipline searching for the dynamics of the interpersonal, it is quite understandable when we hear the question sharply put: Why should theology be here at all? What useful knowledge might it have to offer the study of the interpersonal? What business does theology have outside the boundaries of its own (presumed) area of competence? Why not leave the study of the interpersonal to the psychologists, the sociologists, the psychotherapists, and others?

Immediately we are up against the question of the validity of theology itself—whether it is amenable to consensual validation, whether it offers reliable knowledge, whether its talk about God is talk about anything comprehensible at all. Without yielding to the temptation to be defensive and try to rehearse all the answers that have been given to these questions, I would at least like to account for theology's long-standing and necessary interest in the realm of the interpersonal and why a theology of personal transactions is a job worth doing (in fact, well worth redoing in our particular historical setting), and why it is irresponsible to leave the task entirely to our companion scientific and humanistic disciplines.

Thus I am led to propose: *If God is revealed in history, and if history also includes its end, and if the meaning of history is not understandable apart from its end, and if the end of history is anticipated in the Christ event, as Christian worship celebrates, and if theology's task is to speak, in whatever language is available to it, of God's own self-revelation in history,*[18] then *theology is searching for more inclusive metaphors for grasping the human condition than are its partner disciplines upon whom it depends for discreet data on the human condition.* It is not in the interest of theology's task to deny other modes of grasping the interpersonal, but rather to search for a more holistic mode in which other metaphors can be more adequately grasped. Since the whole of history (including its beginning and end) is the subject of theology's interest, it is in search of the most embracing analogies through which to illuminate the human condition. The Christian community has been grasped by the self-disclosure of God at the end of history in a way that it believes offers the possibility for holistic interpersonal analogies.

1. *Phenomenology*, as a companion discipline to theology in the quest for the interpersonal, is both a significant resource for theological reflection and distinguishable from theology. A phenomenology of personal transactions would seek to describe the transaction without preconditioning assumptions about it. While theology values careful, specific description of the phenomena of personal transactions, it wishes also to bring to the phenomena its memory of the promise of God, and the mighty acts of God in history upon which that promise is based. Thus, while freely using and appreciating phenomenology's lucid descriptions of one-to-one encounter, theology wishes at the same time (and without undercutting the descriptive process) to grasp human encounter under the analogy of the divine-human encounter.

2. *Psychology*, as a companion discipline to theology in the analysis of personal transactions, is both a basic resource for interpersonal theology and distinguishable from the task of theology. Significant models of transactional psychology have been developed by Berne, Homans, Schutz, Thibaut and Kelley, Carson, Leary, Sullivan, and others.[19] They have constructed systems for analyzing preferred behavioral styles, ego states, games, scripts, interpersonal pathology, and therapy. In fact, an enormous fund of literature and data have been produced at an accelerating rate by psychologists in the last two decades. A theology of personal transactions must not neglect these vast and stimulating resources.

While valuing these resources, however, such a theology will be searching for larger metaphors to understand the dynamics of the interpersonal. While freely assimilating and using these systems of interpersonal diagnosis, analysis, and treatment, a transactional theology will be asking about covenant fidelity with the neighbor in the presence of the covenant God who makes himself known in history. This question, I believe, is not extraneous to or intrusive upon the questions of psychological analysis, but is rather a meaningful and necessary intensification of those questions.

3. *Ethics*, as a partner discipline in the study of the interpersonal, is both a welcome companion of theological reflection and yet distinguishable from it. One might argue that what occurs between persons might finally be boiled down to a study of ethics, insofar as ethics takes as its specific concern the values and conflicts of value, the norms and con-

flicted norms, of persons seeking to move toward self-actualization.[20] Such a position neither theology nor psychology can dismiss lightly. For who can deny that at the base of interpersonal conflict lie differences in value or in valuational perspectives of the parties in conflict? Although these may be labeled superego or Parent by the psychologist, they remain as decisive issues in their own right.

An ethic of interpersonal relationships will set itself to the task of analyzing the "oughts," the sense of obligation, the understandings of the good, the normative assumptions, the virtues, the character and justice of persons in encounter. While valuing and using such analyses of moral judgments that lie at the base of interpersonal conflict, a theology of personal transactions will seek to place the human moral judgment within the frame of reference of the judgment of God, the experience of oughtness within the context of the claim of God, and the pursuit of human goods within the context of the Source of all created goods.

4. *Sociology,* social psychology, cultural anthropology, and strategic interaction analysis, as partners in the study of the interpersonal realm, are all useful to a theology of personal transactions and distinguishable from it. A sociology of interpersonal relationships will inquire into the social and institutional determinants of personal transactions, their relation to class stratification, social mobility, social roles, ideologies, ethnicity, and various strata of cultural history. While valuing and using these analyses of the sociocultural environments in which one-to-one encounters occur, a theology of personal transactions will try to place the questions of personal transactions in the even larger frame of reference of purpose and destiny of history, of the covenant of God with humanity, and of the claim of God upon human social constructs.

5. *Law* and jurisprudence, as companions to theology in the study of just relationships, are similarly companions to the theology of personal transactions and yet distinguishable from theology. No tradition has given more attention to the give and take of contractual relationships than has the law. Its case method has developed a comprehensive style of reasoning about rules of justice and equity in relationships where goods and services are exchanged. Detailed legal reasoning spells out how contracts can be validated as binding relationships with the power

of enforcement behind them, and how parties can justly proceed under constituted law when contracts are faulted.

Without denying the wisdom and substance of that legal transactional tradition, transactional theology wants to apply a broader analogy to those contracts, so that the contract between man and man is grasped in the light of the covenant between God and man. The audacity of theology is that it presumes to speak of God's own binding covenant with humanity in such a way that the covenants between person and person are deepened and intensified.

6. *Other disciplines* as well are steady companions in the quest for the understanding of the interpersonal, including history, philosophy, linguistics, literature, political science, the arts, classics, economics, and others in various ways. It is not necessary for us to detail further the shape of the analogies between these efforts and theology's task, inasmuch as they would have the same essential momentum of the previous analogies and thus with some imagination can be easily extrapolated.

I have tried to show theology's relative interdependence with and relative independence from other companion disciplines in the quest for the interpersonal. It is far from my intent, however, to suggest that theology presumes some high status among those disciplines, since its limitations are all too evident. It is to the interest of theology joyfully to disown any pretence to play the "queen of the sciences", and more in keeping with its own mission to view itself as servant of the sciences of man.

In rendering its service, it is called to remember constantly the limits of this service. For theology uses language that is inadequate to its task, if its task is to speak in some sense of the wholeness of history, of the giver and ground of history, of the end toward which history is moving. All it has for such a task is fragile human speech, memory, and reason. Theology can never easily say what it wants to say, or give adequate language to its vision. It can behold it, celebrate it, and in an act of intuitive doxology stand in its glory, but to translate it adequately into human language or propositional statement seems more than language can bear. That is structured into the problem of theologizing itself. That is why the *logos* of theology is necessarily a *doxa-logos* and its reasoning a *para-doxa*.[21]

The History of Transactional Language

The rich interrelationship of history, language, and theology is seen in the problem to which we next turn. I begin with the following hypothesis: *The history of transactional language has already been impacted theologically.* The Christ event is the transaction par excellence, not only in Christian worship, but in the historical memory stored in western languages.

Our talk about a theology of personal transactions will be instructed by probing historically for sharper definitions of the two major terms: transactions and personal.

THE CHRIST EVENT AS PROTOTYPE OF A TRANSACTION

The earliest roots of the English word "transaction" and its Latin antecedents are set in two communities of discourse, law and theology.

The legal-contractual stratum. In Roman civil law a *transactio* referred to an agreement, a settlement of conflicting claims, a covenant, or an adjustment of a dispute between two parties by mutual concession. *Transactio* included not only the covenant duly arrived at, but also the process by which it was hammered out. The emphasis, however, falls upon the conclusion of the agreement. This is seen most clearly in the dual makeup of the word: *trans* (to go beyond or through) *actus* (an action or act of public business). A transaction, therefore, is on the other side of an action. It goes beyond the process of debate or negotiation to agreement. Its public character is seen in the fact that *actus* is used not only for public business but also to denote a public play, a recital, or performance. *Transactio* has the nuance of *driving through* a negotiation to its settlement. It involves the give-and-take exchange of mutual and conflicting interests.

The Christological stratum. The second linguistic tradition is theology. For medieval theology took the legal construct of *transactio* and transmuted it Christologically. Accordingly, *the Christ event became the prototypical transactional event in the western memory.*

The atonement, according to the mainstream of medieval theology, was the final once-and-for-all settlement of the long-standing dispute between God and man. It marked the constituting of a new covenant. It was God's way of dealing finally with sinful man. In the atonement, the God-man drives through *(transactum)* to accomplish a settlement, otherwise impossible, between the righteousness of God and the unrighteousness of man. Thus the Christ event becomes the transaction par excellence in the English language and all Latin-derived languages.

So when we are talking about a theology of personal transactions we are not *introducing* theology afresh into the discussion, but rather we are *remembering* that theological understandings are already impacting on the secular understandings of transactions. It is in this way that the Christ event is crucially embedded into the history of the very concept of a transaction. For in both medieval Latin and early English the Christ event represents the decisive point at which God transacts with history.

The Anselmic definition. The Anselmic form of transactional theology is the most influential model of viewing the God-man encounter as a transaction.[22] The essential argument is as follows: Anselm raises the question, *Cur deus homo?* (Why did God become man?) The question is rooted in the tragic fallenness of human history. Because of his sin, man is not able to give God the satisfaction due him. Anselm presupposed the ancient legal maxim, *poena aut satisfactio* (an offence against justice must either be punished or satisfied).

Mercifully, God does not pursue the way of punishment, as man deserves. If he had, human history would long ago have been annihilated. Yet the satisfaction required of man is far more than he can require, so incredibly has he offended the holiness and justice of God. If spiritually bankrupt man is unable to pay the satisfaction, then, if it is to be done at all, God must do it himself. Yet the essence of the problem is that the satisfaction still must be made by a man, since man is guilty.

The dilemma: It is necessary for man to render satisfaction since man is guilty, and yet fallen man is incapable of rendering the satisfaction. The Anselmic solution: God becomes man. The God-man therefore renders the satisfaction for man, since he is truly man. In this way the incarnation becomes the only possible resolution to the human predicament. What happens in the atonement is described as a *transaction*, and in fact the only conceivable transaction, that could resolve the great dispute between the holy God and sinful man.

The analogical task. We have discussed two levels of tradition through which our transactional language has been mediated to us, the legal-contractual and the theological. Now we ask: How shall contemporary theology proceed to reflect upon both of these strata constructively?

A contemporary theology of personal transactions will reflect on the significant analogies between these two strata, between the divine-human transaction and the transactions between person and person. It will proceed by analogy,[23]—attempting to understand both similarities and differences—between the business level of persons working through mutual claims and conflicting interests and the theological level of God's claims and interests and dealings with humankind. It is amid the dual nuances, ambiguities, and analogies of these two strata of language that a theology of personal transactions will find its arena of work. The analogical method, however, is not merely an attempt to point out similarities, but also differences. For if the two strata are alike in every way, they are not analogous, but rather identical. In order to qualify as an analogy, the two strata must be alike, yet different. We propose that they are different in their similarities and therefore lend themselves to significant analogical reflection.

It is in this way that a contemporary transactional theology will seek to reappropriate the notion of transaction anew as a theological construct, utilizing both the newly bestowed resources of scientific inquiry into interpersonal collusion and intimacy and the traditional theological models of covenant, atonement, and the divine-human encounter.

Thus interpersonal theologizing in a secular context is not just a matter of abstract speculation or archaic confession. Rather, it is among other things a matter of linguistic analysis and historical understanding. The fact that modern men in a secularizing world view may not consciously think of the divine-human transaction when they use the concept of transaction does not change the fact that the word itself has a profound history that quietly impacts upon our secular usages of it and that points paradigmatically to God's own eschatological dealings with man.

My remaining task in discussing the history of transactional language is to probe the term "personal," asking especially how the secularized concept of the personal has *already* been decisively impacted by Judeo-Christian anthropology and theology. My thesis is that the history of language of the person has emerged under the tutelage of trinitarian theology and classical patristic Christology. We will search for a deeper grasp of interpersonal communion by inquiring into the history of personal language, with special concern for the theological stratum of that history.

The structure of personal language. Most languages distinguish between the personal and the impersonal, between I and it, between persons and things. This is not surprising, since language is being called to reflect the reality of the human situation.

Our grammatical structures necessarily distinguish between the person who is speaking (first person), the person spoken to (second person) and the person or thing spoken of (third person). Note that it is principally in the third person that the subpersonal realm enters. (The third person is the realm of objectification). One might schematize this as follows:

> I-I speech is *intra*personal
> I-You speech is *inter*personal
> I-It speech is *sub*personal
> I-Thou speech is *trans*personal

In *The Structure of Awareness* I have developed these four categories more fully. They reflect the four basic existential relationships that constitute the essential context of human relationships (that is to say, any relationship in which one exists may be seen as one of those four modes, or some combination of them).[24] The English word "personal" carries well the nuances of I-I, I-you, and I-Thou, but not I-it language.

The *intimus* character of personalist language is well illustrated in the notion of a "personal reputation," which refers to that collection of virtues or vices associated with a particular person by common consent.

A person's character is knowable only as it emerges in the history of his interactions with his companions. Similarly the notion of a "personal remark" points to the *intimus* level present in the notion of the personal. If A makes a "personal remark" or a personal judgment toward or about B, he is talking about what he perceives to be B's character, his expected conduct, his motivation, his private self as viewed from the outside. Similarly, a *personal transaction*, as I view the term, occurs when something personal is given, received, or withheld.

2. *The theological stratum.* There is another layer of meaning, however, embedded in personalist language. Our common word "person" has been delivered to us through a complex history that has been decisively shaped by trinitarian thought. I would go one step further to assert that personalist language, however secularly used, is not fully understandable without these theological nuances, and in fact has not been delivered to us apart from this theological history.[25]

The Greek word *hypostasis* (literally, substance) was used by Aristotle and the Neoplatonists to refer to objective reality as opposed to illusion. Even in New Testament times this seems to be roughly its meaning, along with the connotation of basis or foundation (Hebrews 1:3, 3:14, 11:1; 2 Corinthians 9:4, 11:17). This is the word, however, which the developing trinitarian thought of the first five centuries took over and began to transmute into the notion of person. From the middle of the fourth century onward, and especially in Christological discussions, *hypostasis* was used to refer to the three persons of the trinity, or "three Hypostaseis in one Ousia."[26]

The central theme of trinitarian thought is that the one God exists in three persons and one substance. Strictly speaking, this doctrine is held to be a mystery, in that it cannot be fully grasped by natural reason apart from revelation, nor can it be adequately demonstrated by reason after it has been revealed. Yet, even though the mystery transcends reason, it is not contrary to reason, according to the teaching of the Church Fathers. In classical trinitarian thought, the perfection of personality is attributed to God.

The term "person" was used further to refer to the person of Christ as uniting the two natures, divine and human. The Council of Chalcedon borrowed another Greek term, *prosopon* (a role, a mask, a character or personage), to point toward Christ's person as divine and human, truly God and truly man, perfect both in deity and in humanness. Accordingly, "both natures concur in one 'person' *(prosōpon)* and in one *hypostasis.* They are not divided or cut into two *prosōpa,* but are together the one and only begotten Logos of God"[27]—the heart of classical Christology.

I hope this detail has not caused the main point of this linguistic excursus to be forgotten: When we employ the construct of the personal in contemporary discussion, we are not introducing theology *de novo* into the notion of the personal, but rather are calling to mind the historical fact that our own secular language of the personal has *already* been decisively impacted by these trinitarian and Christological understandings of the person.

8. Toward a Realistic Interpersonalism

The Paradoxical Structure of Personhood

Christian interpersonal thought from Augustine to Niebuhr beholds the personal transaction as involved in the paradox of human existence, in the sense that the person stands both in and above nature. The transaction exists in time, through causal chains, bound by the limits of natural and bodily existence, yet both partners have the capacity for imagination, reason, and freedom so as to grasp their situation in ways that transcend their purely natural determinants. It is precisely this paradoxical condition of personhood that frustrates any attempt to package neatly a realistic interpersonalism. For all interpersonal meeting is enmeshed in both natural limitation and the capacity for self-transcendence.[1]

Judeo-Christian interpersonalism struggles against a naturalism, on the one hand, that would try to reduce the elements of interpersonal encounter to natural, empirical, behavioral, causal data. On the other hand, it resists the temptation of idealistic romanticism to ignore the natural limitations of personal meeting and overstate the human potentiality. Realistic philosophies of the interpersonal have always faced the

120

challenge of fully accounting for this paradoxical tension that constitutes the essence of personal meeting and more profoundly the human condition.

The paradoxical structure of personhood may be seen from the following two-column delineation. Personhood, and thus interpersonal meeting, is *both*:

Nature	Spirit
Enmeshed in causality	Capable of self-direction
Necessity	Freedom
Limited by natural factors	Capable of self-transcendence
Body	Soul
Existence in time	Present to the eternal
Finite	Infinite
Animal	Rational
Passion	Imagination
Instinct	Cultural creation

In interpersonal meeting, persons confront the paradox that they live both as children of nature and yet they transcend nature through spirit. In meeting the neighbor we discover, on the one hand, that we are compelled by necessities, driven by impulses, constricted by temporal and physical boundaries; above all we remain finite, limited creatures who suffer and must finally face death. Yet to describe the meeting with the neighbor only in terms of these limiting factors is to view human existence from a limited angle. For, on the other hand, human companions are also distinguished from animals who are simply caught in necessity by virtue of the fact that persons can transcend their temporal limits in imagination and control their natural impulses to a certain degree through reason. They have the capacity for self-consciousness and empathy, for an awareness of history, for language, for doxology — in short, for self-transcendence.[2]

It is this essentially contradictory nature of personhood that cunningly and sometimes tragically comes into play in personal transactions and confounds every oversimplified description of a given interaction. Thus our quarrel with simple empirical descriptions of interpersonal behavior is that they often do not do justice to those aspects of interpersonal existence that transcend causal necessity, finitude, and libidinal energies.

If we are to be accountable to the transaction itself, we must go beyond naturalistic description to deal with human self-determination, reason, and freedom in the relationship. Such analyses—for example, Desmond Morris's *The Naked Ape* and Robert Ardrey's *The Territorial Imperative* —are instructive in the sense that they correct our idealistic overexpectations about transactions.[3] But they are, in the long run, only half the truth, since they tend to reduce human social existence to analogies with animal sociality while ignoring the capacity for self-consciousness and self-transcendence.

Our quarrel on the other side, however, is with excessively idealistic descriptions of interpersonal virtues[4] that neglect the animal, passionate, aggressive, libidinal, erotic, and bodily dimensions of personal encounter. These need the correction of a more thoroughgoing naturalistic description of behavioral causes.

Among the *natural* factors that shape the realm of interpersonal meeting are family, nation, race, sexuality, and territoriality. These natural forces paradoxically bring us together in natural bonds of kinship and affection, and yet, as human history has tragically discovered so often, they also have the capacity to separate man from woman, tribe from tribe, our side from their side. In tension with these natural elements stands the *self-transcending* capacity that reaches out for others in intimacy and warmth precisely beyond the boundaries of race, kin, sexuality, and territory. Much of the romantic literature of the world beholds with wonder the capacity for significant interpersonal exchange precisely beyond and in spite of these natural differences (e.g., Romeo and Juliet, whose love reached beyond familial antagonisms). And finally, it should not be forgotten that enspirited humankind, with reason and imagination, can envision possibilities for community that transcend all natural limits in an inclusive, universal society of compassion, freedom, openness, and love for all being (as we find in Augustine, Maimonides, Francis, Kant, and the Baal Shem Tov).

It is precisely this paradoxical nature of personhood that gives rise to the search for the transcendent unity of all things, and thus to religious consciousness. Since human companions are essentially nature and spirit, they are forever homeless in either nature or spirit, and know their homelessness, and therefore search for an understanding of the whole that transcends the nature-spirit tension. In our need for security, we become aware of values dear to us that we characteristically then come to overvalue so as to create idolatries out of limited goods, false gods out of good things, and yet our capacity for spirit leaves us continually dissatisfied with the gods we make for ourselves.

Alienation in Interpersonal Meeting

Interpersonal alienation arises within the paradoxical tension between necessity and freedom, finitude and transcendence, nature and spirit. That tension is not in itself evil, but it does make for the disruption of interpersonal meeting. The paradoxical nature of personhood is the precondition and occasion for sin, but not the cause of it. For our creaturehood (rooted precisely in nature and spirit) is essentially good, but its paradoxical character gives rise to the temptation to sin against our companions in one of two different directions: (1) by sensuality, which seeks inordinately to secure itself in nature, and (2) by a pride that imagines it can divest itself of natural limitations. These two opposite temptations are apparently rooted in the very structure of human existence, and may be seen as latent in every personal transaction.

THE TEMPTATIONS OF INTERPERSONAL MEETING

The temptation to finitize interpersonal meeting. Understandably, a person is tempted on the one hand to seek security at the expense of his neighbor, and so affirm his radical dependence upon nature as to deny his moral accountability to his companions. (This might be called the temptation to finitize, following Kierkegaard.)[5] We all experience the contingencies that go with existing within the boundaries of time and space, and being subject to accident and death. Thus we want to secure ourselves against suffering, discomfort, and deprivation during the brief time we are allotted on this earth, even if it is at the expense of our moral consciousness, which calls us to be accountable to a higher vision of human community. The press for security tempts us all to repress that part of our humanness which is self-transcending and has its home beyond the hedonic and natural. This temptation is latent in every human transaction.

The temptation to infinitize interpersonal meeting. We are tempted, on the other hand, in personal transactions to imagine that we can escape natural limitations. We pretend to be so free, so reasonable, so purely spirit that these natural contingencies are not present for us. (Kierkegaard called this "the despair of infinitude.")[6] It leads us to imagine that in our personal meeting we need not be bound by these wretched and embarrassing limitations of time and space. Ultimately it may lead to a perfectionism that entices the individual to think that his actions within this world already have the character of finality. Thus a part of our paradoxical nature, the self-transcending dimension, is always waiting in the wings in any personal encounter to tempt the individual to imagine that he can fully and finally transcend his natural limitations.

Every occasion of personal meeting in this way presents me with the occasion for sin against my own nature and against my neighbor. For we both stand at the juncture between nature and spirit. We are tempted to collude with each other so as to hook into each other's needs to overidealize or overly secure our existence. The structure of human existence preconditions interpersonal sin, but sin finally remains our choice, and is not necessitated by the structure of human existence, a point that will receive further development.

SIN AS INEVITABLE, BUT NOT NECESSARY

In the biblical witness, persons do not simply originate evil out of their own individual will. It always has an interpersonal character. It emerges in dialogue, and ordinarily in response to a tempter. The temptation is symbolized in the Bible by mythic and demonic images—serpents, Satan, etc. The tempter ordinarily has the nuance that sin is a mysterious offer that comes to the person as an attractive alternative over against the order of existence given by God. That order, of course, is a fragile, paradoxical order that is quite easily, it seems, misconceived or abused.

It is in this way that the human condition inevitably tempts collusive partners to pride and/or sensuality, by the negation of either their finitude or their possibilities. And yet, if it is inevitable that transactions are always tempted toward inauthenticity in one or the other of these two directions, then how can it be maintained that persons are free and thus responsible for their behavior?

The dynamics of collusion lead the realistic observer to conclude that there is profound wisdom in the classical religious formulation of the notion of original sin, which without denying freedom sees the conditions of existence as tending inevitably toward corruption and loss of its original (paradoxical) balance. Yet its inevitability does not reduce the level of human responsibility, since it is always the free person who responds freely to the temptation. This leads Reinhold Niebuhr to conclude perceptively that sin is "inevitable but not necessary,"[7] i.e., the very structure of human existence tends to make it inevitable that persons fall into pride and sensuality, and thus the condition of interpersonal sin is apparently universal in all human transactions, and yet it is not necessitated by the nature of personhood, which always freely colludes with the tempting possibility.

When Christian interpersonalism speaks about a defect of the will that tends in any given transaction to be ready to be tempted to pride or sensuality, that is still a major step away from admitting a naturally evil will that might be thought to be a part of the constituted definition of personhood, which would be an unbearable offence to the Christian doctrine of persons as creatures, created in the image of God, and of God's creation as fundamentally good. Thus, although sin is inevitable in interpersonal meeting, its very inevitability points us toward the existential freedom that is a constant component of its inevitability. Again, Reinhold Niebuhr has formulated the paradox concisely by saying that the person "is most free in the discovery that he is not free."[8]

Power in Personal Relationships

THE DYNAMICS OF INTERPERSONAL POWER

(a) *The neglect of power.* Collusions of various forms of dominance and submissiveness are well-known factors in the dynamics of interpersonal behavior. The central tradition of interaction analysis from Leary, through Thibaut and Kelley, to Carson,[9] views the dominant-submissive pole as one of the essential elements of any personal transaction. A Christian interpersonalism must incorporate a realistic analysis of power into its perspective without failing to keep power in tension with justice and love.

The relation of person to person may appropriately be understood as a relation of power to power. Interpersonal freedom involves the power to be, to engage, to enter into relation, the power to withdraw, to reject, to collude and to support.[10]

Generally speaking, power is a neglected theme in religious discussions of the interpersonal, the result of which has been that the religious critique has not been taken seriously by behavioral scientists, who are much clearer about the importance of interpersonal power in the marketing of potentially complementary personal transactions.[11] Idealistic social thought generally has tended to neglect power and conflict, and particularly in its exaggerated utopian and pacifist forms it has doggedly refused to acknowledge the moral dimensions of power. The realistic interpersonalism which I am seeking to outline here stands in tension both with humanistic optimisms, which would neglect the dynamics of power in interpersonal meeting and with crass Machiavellian interpretations of sociality, which see interactions *only* as expressions of power, and thus fail to grasp the self-transcending and spiritual elements of intersubjectivity.

(b) *The balance and organization of interpersonal power.* Personal transactions thus may be viewed as a negotiation of the power of natural interests and the power of spirit. I might say, on the one hand, that a particular interaction can be viewed "from below," as it were, as an equilibrium of competing interests that without organization tends toward anarchy and sheer individualistic passion.[12]

The transaction may also be viewed "from above," where rationality, data-gathering, Adult reality orientation, and structure hunger are striving for order, organization, and cohesiveness. There is a tendency in any sustained transactional sequence to search for norms that will stabilize and structure the relationship so that it might be less prone to the abuse of libidinal energies and uncontrolled self-interest. Thus the dyad searches for routinized ways of making just relationships normative. They calculate their interests in a longer time frame, developing customs, laws, and organization aimed at achieving harmony in personal meeting. If a relationship is to be sustained through time it must have some sort of rational organization of roles and implicit definition of contracts, even though that rationality is never free from passionate impulse and abuse. Reason and imagination are never able so fully to order mutual interests that their flow is fully controlled.[13]

Thus these two elements, the balance of power and the organization of power, are at work in any given transactional sequence so that it may be viewed from below or from above. Without rational and normative organization, transactions tend to become capricious and unjust. Without some mutuality of interests being exchanged, transactions tend to truncate and fall apart, no matter how much effort is given to trying to hold them together through rational organization.

(c) *Political analogies.* These two ways of viewing dyadic interpersonal meeting are analogous with two broader positions in social philosophy. The view of interaction "from below" corresponds in western social philosophy to the tradition of social realism from Machiavelli through the utilitarian and laissez-faire theorists to contemporary theorists of the balance of power. Anarchism is its most extreme philosophical expression. The most justifiable criticism of this tradition has been its failure to grasp the necessity of the orderly rationalization of conflicting interests.

The view of interaction "from above" corresponds in western social philosophy to the tradition of social idealism from Grotius through philosophical idealism, socialism, and various brands of collectivism. This tradition trusts reason to create just order. The most justifiable criticism of this tradition is its tendency to impose excessive organization unjustly and artificially on social forces so as to limit and constrict their natural vital balance.

These two opposing tendencies in social philosophy correspond to the basic tension in the paradoxical nature of man; in fact, they are political expressions of the opposite temptations to sensuality and pride.

INTERPERSONAL JUSTICE

American religious thought tends to be irrelevant to personal transactions because it typically focuses upon the absolute demand for perfect love to the neglect of the accommodation of interests in interpersonal conflict. When we try to substitute absolute love for relative justice in the interpersonal realm, we fail to understand the power of self-interest that is present as much in the lives of the religious as it is in the secular.

The task of interpersonal justice is to resist the excessive claims of self-interest in personal transactions. It assumes that power is certain to be expressed in interpersonal meeting and it therefore searches for ways of protecting legitimate claims while resisting excessive self-assertion.

The relation between love and justice,[14] long a hinge of Christian ethics, bears significantly on interpersonal theology. Love rises above justice in personal relationships to exceed its demand, but it does not abrogate the demand for justice. Justice is love taking shape under the conditions of human estrangement. The rules of justice attempt to make concrete and implement the demands of love. Justice does not merely follow the inspiration of the spirit in the moment, but seeks to define expected behaviors and systems of relationships through which love might express itself in complex social arrangements. In doing so, it takes fully into account the natural self-interest of the person and the neighbor. Thus a Christian transactional ethic cannot be based simply on agape, the perfect self-sacrificial love of the cross, but, rather, it is also concerned with a mutual and conditional love that seeks to translate itself into justice in interpersonal meeting.

Although agape may be present and experienced in certain peak moments of interpersonal meeting, we cannot reasonably expect such love to be the sustained basis of interaction, since sacrificial love involves the disavowal of power. Justice at the interpersonal level seeks an equitable ordering of power in the light of mutual self-interest. Justice is not capable of bestowing upon personal transactions the conditions of ideality and perfection. It may give more concreteness to love under the conditions of human estrangement, however, than could a purer idealism.

The problem with most traditional theories of justice, whether in their classical, Thomistic, or rationalistic forms, is that they are often unaware of the conditioned, historically relative character of human reasoning. With few exceptions, theorists of justice have not demonstrated the capacity to grasp the relativity of justice without undercutting the very ground and nature of justice itself.

Christ on the cross reveals the character of love as radical self-giving while at the same time revealing man's lovelessness and the destructiveness of his self-interest. While Christian worship celebrates the radical self-giving love of God as the final claim upon the interpersonal realm —and in fact the highest possibility of man—nonetheless, it does not cease to hope for the equitable adjustment of interests in ordinary transactions. If the cross shows us anything, it shows us that in history pure sacrificial love is crucified.[15]

Epilogue: The Hunger for Intimacy and the Limits of the Encounter Culture

Few items stand higher on the agenda of crucial issues in our society than that of finding a way to be real with others, of learning to relate openly and intimately to people we love and are in tension with. Among persons whom I have come to know well, I experience a profound hunger for interpersonal meeting, for honesty and clarity in interpersonal communication. There is a driving thirst in our emerging culture for what might be called interpersonal authenticity[2]—being oneself in the presence of others. I have no doubt that such a hunger has also been present or latent in other cultural settings and historical periods. But in the current cultural setting it is evident and unmistakable.

The evidence that is most persuasive to me is not merely the flourishing of small group processes questing for personal honesty and closeness,[2] but that precisely the persons who have experienced such groups on a short-term basis now find themselves searching for more sustained relationships of interpersonal authenticity in their daily lives, their vocational spheres, their marriage relationships and their families and friends.[3] This is the so-called reentry problem following the intensive group experience.

The eerie, disquieting phenomenon of the drug culture, which reached its peak and has been receding since the early 1970s, has impacted deeply on our consciousness. It expressed a disillusionment with a plastic society and a hunger for expanded consciousness through chemistry.[4]

Ironically, it may be becoming evident from the viewpoint of the Hebraic understanding of history that God has been at work even in the drug culture, calling us toward community and interpersonal accountability. For the drug culture has had the unexpected consequence of drawing us closer together, since the horrifying possibilities of the drug experience have tended to awaken the need for social cohesion and deeper intimacy.[5]

The renewed quest for the interpersonal took new momentum during this period of exceptional alienation in our society. We discovered that we did not know how to experience others. Drugs did not seem to help. The drug culture remains a severe indictment of depersonalizing culture. Yet in the rebound from that period there has been an intensification of the search for intimacy.[6]

When I listen carefully to persons around me, I hear a hunger, a cry, and an outrage—a quiet hunger for interpersonal communion, a cry for interpersonal accountability, and an outrage against the depersonalization so familiar to us all. Much social momentum resists the formation of abiding personal friendships. We find ourselves pitted against each other in competitive power struggles, deceptive games, and manipulative ploys. The environment of postindustrial man seems especially poorly designed for personal intimacy.[7]

Where are intimates being portrayed, for example, in the contemporary theater? Look over a sampling of the stock of characters in recent drama: the Arthur Miller characters (Willie, Biff, Happy, Maggie, the Proctors); the Tennessee Williams characters (Stan, Blanche, Big Daddy, Brick, Chance, Amanda); the Edward Albee characters (George, Martha, Mother and Daddy, Alice); the Harold Pinter characters (Petey, Meg, Gus, Goldberg); the Samuel Beckett characters (Vladimir,

Estragon, Clov, Hamm, Nagg, Krapp). Almost none of them experience intimacy.

The message I derive from this is twofold: The contemporary theater is showing us profoundly the hunger for intimacy and the absence of intimacy in contemporary life; and theater as a mode of communication is revealed here in its limitation, since dramatic conflict, if credible, must deal with interpersonal alienation. It is easier for the theater to focus upon the dynamics of the lack of intimacy than to picture self-actualizing forms of intimacy, just as psychology has found it easier to understand pathology than health.

Why is it so urgent in our society to rediscover the wellsprings of interpersonal health? We exist day by day in an environment of structured distance between people in a "temporary" soceity amid accelerating mobility. We meet, come together for a short time, and soon go our separate ways. This has created a "throwaway" society, where relationships tend to be manipulative, rootless, and ruthless.

Urban planners are now questing for a village scale *within* the city. They are belatedly trying to recover a smaller scale for personal transactions within the larger scale of the city. Only too tardily have they got around to responding to a silently growing need of many for personal authenticity in compacted environments.

The strength of the encounter culture is the short-term intensive group experience. In fact, it is ironically not too difficult in our society to obtain a relationship of relative honesty and quasi-intimacy on a short-term basis through intensive group processes. Far from putting them down, I see these experiences as a positive effort, however inadequate and class-limited, to speak to a profound need in our society for interpersonal authenticity. A dozen people get together for a 48-hour marathon. They may have never seen each other before. They will not see each other again. Yet they may achieve a remarkable sense of confession, mutual care, self-affirmation and closeness for those 48 hours. The purpose of the process is to simulate some of the conditions of intimacy. But then they go back to their ordinary environments and find themselves locked into role relationships in which they may find exceptional difficulty "being themselves."

Many people today are looking for means of sustaining interpersonal authenticity for more than a few hours. They are looking for filial, fraternal, and friendship relationships they can count on as trustworthy, not just for two weeks, but for twenty years, or for a lifetime. Here Alvin Toffler[8] badly miscalculated the shape of the future as increasingly mobile. On the contrary, what I see ahead is the need for re-rootage, the deceleration of mobility, and a new search for moral accountability that will look to some like a "new puritanism."

We are mourning the loss of integrity, of personal reliability, of sustained responsibility in personal dealings. I admit to a certain nostalgia about the small southwestern town in which I grew up, where everything seemed to be together, where a man's word was his bond, where there was little social mobility (that is probably the reason I left); and yet precisely because of that lack of mobility, relationships seemed to be more trustworthy, less manipulative, more fixed and stable, more palpable. Plato's ideal of the size of the *polis*[9] was very near the size of my home town. It seemed that everybody knew everybody else, and that no one could have possibly existed there whom no one knew about or failed to recognize. Although I surely must idealize it, I think it seemed clear to most everyone that the people they lived with would be the people they would have to deal with until the day they died. This gave a certain substance to covenants and reputations and interactions. There was a clear line drawn between those who lived in the town and those who came through, not in the sense of rejection of newcomers (usually they were heartily welcomed), but rather in the sense of an implicit knowledge that those whom you could really count on were those with whom you were committed to spend the rest of your life.

The encounter culture is a relevant response to the mourning of interpersonal depth, but an incomplete and unstable one. It is a clue to a deeper hunger and alienation in our society. The religious traditions, whose communities still have many remaining elements of social cohesion and still (despite dire predictions) enjoy greater public confidence than educational or governmental institutions, are being called to participate creatively in this quest for interpersonal authenticity. They would seem to be better positioned sociologically to serve a society in need of sustained relationships of personal integrity than are the growth centers, encounter groups, and the endless stream of therapy fads.

What are religious communities being called to do in such an environment? Certainly not to reduce the worshiping community to an encounter group. They are asked to listen clearly to the hunger of humanity, hear the cry for intimacy, study the scientific data available, and bring to bear the wisdom of their traditions upon that body of research. Much that is being learned in group processes can be assimilated (or better, "relearned") by the religious communities.

The Jewish-Christian tradition has in fact had wide historical experience with the intensive group process, as is evident from the fact that basic models for the encounter group have emerged directly from the history of Protestant and Jewish pietism. The religious communities today who are heirs of those traditions are in fact being decisively challenged to develop actual communities which in fact embody the kinds of openness, truth-telling, intimacy and interpersonal virtues of which they so often speak. They are being called not to hide their candle under a bushel, but rather to let the world behold and share in the actual fellowship which the liturgy celebrates.

One thing that religious reflection has not learned to do—and it remains on our agenda—is to grasp in ordinary daily transactions the reality of sin, the presence of God's judgment and grace, and the providential action of God in history, i.e., the elementary categories of Judeo-Christian understanding that are relevant to an understanding of the interpersonal.

The transactional image of give-and-take commodity exchanges in the interpersonal realm is consistent with the Judeo-Christian memory of man's sinfulness, self-assertiveness, and inclination always to guarantee his own interest.[10] That is not all that can be said about man, but it must be said in order to gain credibility in anything else we say about man.

Transactional psychology, heavily oriented toward self-interest, stands in tension with the optimistic assumption that the human will is basically good and history is getting better and better. Too easily we have assumed that the demonic elements in willing can be easily mastered or permissively ignored.

It is geographically and philosophically significant that the human potential movement had its gestation and birth on the far western edge of the American continent—at Big Sur, on the Pacific Ocean. It seems as if we had explored all we could in this country, run out of territory, and then turned to inner space, to the human potential as an area of exploration. Esalen is a pop expression of the doctrine of manifest destiny.

The biblical celebration of God's love and cosmic affirmation does not fail to recognize human pride, self-interest, and deception. Judeo-Christian wisdom is not cheap optimism about the universal love of God for being—period—without also perceiving the tragic alienation of man. In fact, it perceives most sharply the quandaries of humankind precisely in the light of the radical love of God that acts to undermine those quandaries.[11] Faith in God reasons analogically *from* its memory of God's forgiving love *to* human sinfulness, and thereby beholds sinfulness from the vantage point of its having been *de jure* overcome without denying its *de facto* power.

Notes

I. INTERPERSONAL COMMUNION

1. INTIMACY: A DEFINITION

1. *Oxford Universal English Dictionary*, C. T. Onions, ed., Oxford University Press, 1937, 5: 1034.

2. Albert Blaise, ed., *Dictionnaire Latin-Français des Auteurs Chrétiens*, Librairie des Meridiens, 1954, 468. C. T. Lewis and C. Short, *A Latin Dictionary*, Oxford University Press, 1955. R. E. Latham, *Revised Medieval Latin Word List*, Oxford University Press, 1965.

3. Erving Goffman, *The Presentation Self in Everyday Life*, Doubleday, 1959, 208 ff.

4. "This condition may be denoted *crasis*, a genuine interlocking of personalities; or more colloquially, it may be called *intimacy.*" Eric Berne, *Transactional Analysis in Psychotherapy*, Grove Press, 1961 (Hereafter *TAP).*

5. *Webster's Third New International Dictionary*, unabridged, G. & C. Merriam, 1961.

6. Martin Buber, *I and Thou*, trans. Walter Kaufmann, Scribner's, 1970, 55; *Between Man and Man*, Beacon Press, 1955 (hereafter *BMM).*

7. Ross Snyder, *On Becoming Human*, Abingdon Press, 1967, 54 ff.; Reuel L. Howe, *The Miracle of Dialogue*, Seabury, 1963.

8. Howard J. Clinebell, Jr., and Charlotte H. Clinebell, *The Intimate Marriage*, Harper & Row, 1970, 37 ff.

9. George R. Bach and Peter Wyden, *The Intimate Enemy: How to Fight*

Fair in Love and Marriage, Avon, 1968; Eric Berne, *Games People Play*, Grove Press, 1964 (hereafter *GPP*); William Schutz, *Joy: Expanding Human Awareness*, Grove Press, 1967; Alexander Lowen, *Love and Orgasm*, Macmillan, 1965, *Pleasure*, Coward-McCann, 1970; Gerald Goodman, *Companionship Therapy*, Jossey-Bass, 1972; R. M. Mazur, *The New Intimacy*, Beacon Press, 1973.

10. Specifically the instructions were: "Think of a particular relation of genuine intimacy with another person. Call to mind a good friend, close associate, childhood companion, or your spouse—one with whom you have experienced intense emotive reasonance and fulfilling closeness, whose internal reality you have in some sense come to know and love. Let your imagination flow with the experience. Make yourself comfortable; breathe deeply; as you exhale let your muscles relax—around your eyes, mouth, neck, back, arms, pelvis, legs, toes. Experience in memory and imagination what it is like to be there with that person in a moment of warmth and affection. Let that person's facial features appear in your awareness. Recall the particular place, the context in which you felt closest. Be there with your partner. Let that environment frame the face of your partner. Let the feelings flow between you and your partner—whatever feelings are there—do not block them, stay with them. Rehearse in fantasy whatever activity or event you are sharing with your partner. (Pause.) At times there are moments of ecstacy or overflowing feelings with persons with whom we are very close. If you felt such a moment with this person, savor that moment. (Pause.) Now it is time to come back to this group. When you feel like it, open your eyes, and come back and be fully present to this group here and now."

11. For a theoretical discussion of these difficulties, see H. A. Murray, "Toward a Classification of Interaction," in T. Parsons and E. A. Shils, eds., *Toward a General Theory of Action*, Harvard University Press., 1951, 434–464.

12. I have developed this category in *The Structure of Awareness*, Abingdon Press, 1968 (hereafter *SA*), 16 ff., 232 ff.

13. A. H. Maslow, *Toward a Psychology of Being*, Van Nostrand, 1962; *Religions, Values and Peak Experiences*, Viking Press, 1970 (hereafter *TPB* and *RVP*).

14. Cf. Martin Buber, *I and Thou; BMM*, Part I.

15. Genesis 2:234.

16. In this connection see Gabriel Marcel's profound essay, "Presence as a Mystery," in *The Mystery of Being*, Henry Regnery Co., 1950, 1: 242 ff.

17. See Marc Oraison, *Being Together*, Doubleday, 1971, 139 ff; Buber, *The Knowledge of Man*, Harper Torchbooks, 1965, 72 ff.

18. Maslow, *RVP*, 63.

19. See Wayne E. Oates, *Protestant Pastoral Counseling*, *Westminster Press*, 1962, 75 ff.

20. Contra Berne, who speaks of his " 'intimacy experiment' in which two people sit close to each other 'eyeball to eyeball' and keep eye contact while talking straight to each other . . . it demonstrates that any two people of either sex, starting as strangers or mere acquantances, can attain intimacy in fifteen minutes or so under proper conditions." *Sex in Human Loving,* Simon and Schuster, 1970, 117–118 (hereafter *SHL).*

21. Cf. Karl Barth, *Church Dogmatics,* esp. Vol. 4, T. & T. Clark, 1956 ff.; and Paul Ramsey, *Basic Christan Ethics,* SCM Press, 1953, 267 ff.

22. "The Form of Solemnization of Matrimony," *The Book of Common Prayer,* SPCK, n.d., 217.

23. Virginia Satir, *Conjoint Family Therapy,* Science and Behavior Books, 1967. See "Communication: A Verbal and Nonverbal Process of Making Requests of the Receiver," 75 ff. Cf. my essay, "Optimal Conditions for Learning —Toward a Clarification of the Learning Contract," *Religious Education,* March–April 1972.

24. Howe, *Herein Is Love,* Judson Press, 1961.

25. Carl R. Rogers, *Client-Centered Therapy,* Houghton Mifflin, 1951.

26. Robert L. Katz, *Empathy: Its Nature and Uses,* Collier-Macmillan, 1963.

27. Cf. Max Scheler, *The Nature of Sympathy,* Yale University Press, 1954.

28. Thomas C. Oden, *Kerygma and Counseling,* Westminster Press, 1965, 50 ff. (hereafter *KC).*

29. For further lucid discussion of this issue see Don S. Browning, *Atonement and Psychotherapy,* Westminster Press, 1966, 174 ff.

30. Rogers, "A Theory of Therapy, Personality, and Interpersonal Relationships, as Developed in the Client-Centered Framework," in *Psychology: A Study of a Science,* ed. Sigmund Koch, McGraw-Hill, 1959, 206.

31. George R. Bach, "A Theory of Intimate Aggression," *Psychological Report,* 1965, *18,* 449–450.

32. Bach and Wyden, *The Intimate Enemy,* 17–95. Cf. Buber, *I and Thou,* 68.

33. George R. Bach and R. M. Deutsch, *Pairing,* Avon, 1970, 153 ff. Cf. Anthony Storr, *Human Aggression,* Atheneum, 1968.

34. S. Schacter, *The Psychology of Affiliation,* Stanford University Press, 1959.

35. Leonard Campos and Paul McCormick, *Introduce Yourself to Transactional Analysis,* San Joaquin TA Institute, 1969, 18; Eric Berne, *GPP,* 180 ff.

36. See Carl Michalson, *Worldly Theology,* Scribner's, 1967; Oden, *KC,* Chaps. 1, 2.

37. Rogers, *On Becoming a Person,* Houghton Mifflin, 1961, 283.

38. Rogers, *Client-Centered Therapy.*

39. Jack Gibb, "Climate for Trust Formation," in L. P. Bradford, J. R. Gibb, K. E. Benne, eds., *T-Group Theory and Laboratory Method,* John Wiley, 1964; Everett L. Shostrom, *Man, the Manipulator,* Abingdon Press, 1967.

40. Julius Fast, *Body Language,* M. Evans, 1970; Jane Howard, *Please Touch,* McGraw-Hill, 1970.

41. Buber, *Knowledge of Man,* 59 ff. Cf. F. E. Fiedler, "The Psychological-Distance Dimension in Interpersonal Relations," *Journal of Personality,* 1953, *22,* 142–150.

42. Exodus 20:16.

43. Berne, *What Do You Say After You Say Hello?: The Psychology of Human Destiny,* Grove Press, 1972, 444 (hereafter *Hello).*

44. Muriel James and Dorothy Jongeward, *Born to Win: Transactional Analysis with Gestalt Experiments,* Addison-Wesley, 1971, 58 (hereafter *BW).*

45. Sidney M. Jourard, *The Transparent Self: Self-disclosure and Well-being,* Van Nostrand, 1964.

46. Morton Hunt, *The Affair,* New American Library, 1969.

47. Oraison, *Being Together,* 191 ff.; E. Brunner, *The Divine Imperative,* Westminster Press, 1947, Part 3.

48. Erich Fromm, *The Art of Loving,* Harper & Row, 1962.

49. This point has been perceptively developed by Elizabeth O'Conner, *Journey Inward, Journey Outward,* Harper & Row, 1968. See also Dietrich Bonhoeffer, *Life Together,* Harper & Bros., 1954, 40 ff.

50. H. Richard Niebuhr, *Radical Monotheism and Western Culture,* Harper & Bros., 1960. See Oden, *SA,* Part 1.

51. Buber, *The Way of Man,* Wilcox and Follett, 1951; *I and Thou,* 123 ff.; *Believing Humanism,* Simon and Schuster, 1969.

52. Wolfhart Pannenberg, *Basic Questions in Theology,* 2 vols., Fortress Press, 1970, 1971 (hereafter *BQT).*

2. DILEMMAS OF INTIMACY

1. Paul Tournier, *Escape from Loneliness,* Westminster Press, 1948; *The Strong and the Weak,* Westminster Press, 1963.

2. W. Blanchard, "Ecstacy Without Agony Is Baloney," *Psychology Today,* January 1970.

3. Erving Goffman, *Stigma: Notes on the Management of Spoiled Identity,* Prentice-Hall, 1963.

4. J. Nuttin, "Intimacy and Shame in the Dynamic Structure of Personal-

ity," in M. I. Reymert, ed., *Feelings and Emotions*, McGraw-Hill, 1950.

5. Paul Tillich, *The Courage to Be*, Yale University Press, 1952.

6. Clark E. Moustakas, *Individuality and Encounter: A Brief Journey into Loneliness and Sensitivity Groups*, Howard A. Doyle, 1968. See also W. G. Hollister, "Brainwashing vs. Strengthening Individuality," *Human Relations Training News*, 1969, *13* (4), 1.

7. See my discussion, "Choice Demands Negation," *SA*, Part 1.

8. Contra Berne, *GPP*, 35–67, 184 ff.

9. H. R. Niebuhr, *Radical Monotheism and Western Culture*, 114 ff.

10. Soren Kierkegaard, *The Diary*, ed. P. Rohde, Philosophical Library, 1960.

11. Ira J. Tanner, *Loneliness: The Fear of Love*, Harper & Row, 1973; Cf. Tournier, *Escape from Loneliness;* Moustakas, *Individuality and Encounter.*

12. George R. Bach and Ronald M. Deutsch, *Pairing*, Avon, 1970, 13 ff.

13. Rollo May, *Love and Will*, W. W. Norton, 1969.

14. James H. Lapsley, *Salvation and Health*, Westminster Press, 1972, "History of the Salvation-Health Relationship," 31 ff.

15. Paul Bindrim, "Nudity as a Quick Grab for Intimacy in Group Therapy," *Psychology Today*, June 1969, *3* (1); see also portions of Rasa Gustaitis, *Turning On*, Signet, 1970, and Severin Peterson, *A Catalog of the Ways People Grow*, Ballantine, 1971.

16. William Masters and Virginia Johnson, *Human Sexual Response*, Little, Brown, 1966.

17. Albert Ellis and Roger O. Conway, *The Art of Erotic Seduction*, Lyle Stuart, 1967.

18. Vance Packard, *The Sexual Wilderness*, McKay, 1968.

19. Seward Hiltner, *Theological Dynamics*, Abingdon Press, 1972, 125–147. See also *Sex Ethics and the Kinsey Reports*, Association Press, 1953, and *Sex and the Christian Life*, Association Press, 1957.

3. THERAPY AS SURROGATE INTIMACY

1. C. Truax and R. Carkhuff, *Toward Effective Counseling and Psychotherapy: Training and Practice*, Aldine, 1967.

2. Sigmund Freud, *Therapy and Technique*, Collier Books, 1963; cf. Clara Thompson, ed., *An Outline of Psychoanalysis*, Modern Library, 1955, chaps. 28–31.

3. Thomas S. Szasz, *The Ethics of Psychoanalysis*, Dell, 1965, 104 ff; Berne, *Hello*, 443.

4. Berne, *Hello*, 88.

5. The reader will note that many of the studies that support this thesis are the same as those noted in my recent study, *After Therapy What?: Lay Therapeutic Resources in Religious Perspective*, Charles C. Thomas, 1974. Although the intent of these two discussions is quite different, the supportive evidence is substantially similar. The lectures which appear in that volume were delivered in January of 1972.

6. H. Eysenck, "The Effects of Psychotherapy: An Evaluation," *J. Consult. Psychol.*, 1952, *16*, 319–324; see also *The Effects of Psychotherapy*, International Science Press, 1966.

7. Truax and Carkhuff, op. cit., 5.

8. J. Frank, *Persuasion and Healing*, Johns Hopkins Press, 1961.

9. F. Barron and T. Leary, "Changes in Psychoneurotic Patients with and without Psychotherapy," *J. Consult. Psychol.*, 1955, *19*, 239–245.

10. R. Cartwright and J. Vogel, "A Comparison of Changes in Psychoneurotic Patients During Matched Periods of Therapy and No Therapy," *J. Consult. Psychol.*, 1960, *24*, 121–127. O. Mink and H. Isaacson, "A Comparison of Effectiveness of Non-directive Therapy and Clinical Counseling in the Junior High School," *School Counselor*, 1959, *6*, 12–14. L. Gliedman, E. Nash, S. Imber, A. Stone, and J. Frank, "Reduction of Symptoms by Pharmacologically Inert Substances and by Short-term Psychotherapy," *A.M.A. Arch. Neurol. Psychiat.*, 1957, *79*, 345–351. R. Walker and F. Kelley, "Short-term Psychotherapy with Hospitalized Schizophrenic Patients," *Acta Psychiat. Neurol. Scand.*, 1960, *35*, 34–56. J. Barendregt, "A Psychological Investigation of the Effects of Psychoanalysis and Psychotherapy," in J. Barendregt, *Research in Psychodiagnostics*, Mouton, 1961.

11. J. Anker and R. Walsh, "Group Psychotherapy, a Special Activity Program, and Group Structure in the Treatment of Chronic Schizophrenia," *J. Consult. Psychol*, 1961, *25*, 476–481.

12. B. Levitt, "The Results of Psychotherapy with Children: An Evaluation," *J. Consult. Psychol.*, 1957, *21*, 189–196. H. Eysenck, ed., *Behavior Therapy and Neuroses*, Pergamon Press, 1960. J. Matarazzo, "Some Psychotherapists Make Patients Worse!" *International Journal of Psychiatry*, 1967, *3*, 156–157.

13. Truax and Carkhuff, 20–21.

14. A. Bergin, "The Evaluation of Therapeutic Outcomes," in A. Bergin and S. Garfield, eds., *Handbook of Psychotherapy and Behavior Change: An Empirical Analysis*, Wiley, 1971, 217–270.

15. Jerome Agel, *The Radical Therapist*, Ballantine Books, 1971; *Rough Times*, Ballantine Books, 1973.

16. Rogers, "The Necessary and Sufficient Conditions of Therapeutic

Personality Change," *J. Consult. Psych.*, 1957, *21*, 95–103. Carl R. Rogers and Barry Stevens, *Person to Person*, Real People Press, 1967, 85 ff.

17. Truax and Carkhuff, 100.

18. J. C. Whitehorn and B. Betz, "A Study of Psychotherapeutic Relationships Between Physicians and Schizophrenic Patients," *Amer. J. Psychiat.*, 1954, *3*, 321–331. B. Betz, "Differential Success Rates of Psychotherapists with 'Process' and 'Non-process' Schizophrenic Patients," *Amer. J. Psychiat.*, 1963, *11*, 1090–1091.

19. Truax and Carkhuff, 96.

20. Ibid., 108.

21. Ibid., 111.

22. Charles C. Thomas, 1974. Portions of this argument may be found in the *Journal of Humanistic Psychology*, Spring 1974, "A Populist's View of Psychotherapeutic Deprofessionalization."

23. G. Goodman, *Companionship Therapy*, Jossey-Bass, 1972, chap. 1.

24. Ibid., 227.

25. Ibid.

26. Ibid., 28.

27. Ibid., chap. 3.

28. Ibid., chap. 10.

29. B. Berzon, and L. Solomon, "Research Frontier: The Self-directed Therapeutic Group—Three Studies," *J. of Counsel. Psych.*, 1966, *13*, 491–497. O. Mowrer, *The New Group Therapy*, Van Nostrand, 1964. J. Gibb and L. Gibb, "Leaderless Groups: Growth-centered Values and Potentials," in H. Otto and M. Mann, eds., Ways of Growth: Approaches to Expanding Awareness, Grossman, 1968, 101–114. N. Hurvitz, "Peer Self-help Psychotherapy Groups and Their Implications for Psychotherapy," *Psychotherapy: Theory, Research and Practice*, 1970, *7*, 41–49. P. Hanson, P. Rothaus, D. Johnson, and F. Lyle, "Autonomous Groups in Human Relations Training for Psychiatric Patients," *J. of Appl. Behav. Sci.*, 1966 *2* (3), 305 ff. V. G. Zunker and W. F. Brown, "Comparative Effectiveness of Student and Professional Counselors," *Personnel and Guidance Journal*, 1966, *44*, 738–743. W. E. Mitchell, "Amicatherapy: Theoretical Perspectives and an Example of Practice," *Community Mental Health Journal*, 1966a, *2* (4), 307–314. W. E. Mitchell, "The Use of College Student Volunteers in the Out-Patient Treatment of Troubled Children," in H. R. Huessy, ed., *Mental Health with Limited Resources*, Grune & Stratton, 1966, 28–37. T. M. Magoon and S. E. Golann, "Nontraditionally Trained Women as Mental Health Counselors/Psychotherapists," *Personnel and Guidance Journal*, 1966, *44*, 788–792. J. D. Holzberg, R. H. Knapp, and J. L. Turner, "College Students as Companions to the Mentally Ill," in E. L. Cowen, E. A.

Gardner, and M. Zax, eds., *Emergent Approaches to Mental Health*, Appleton-Century-Crofts, 1967. J. D. Holzberg, H. S. Whiting, and D. G. Lowy, "Chronic Patients and a College Companion Program," *Mental Hospitals*, 1964, *15* (3), 152–158. N. B. Patterson, and T. W. Patterson, "A Companion Therapy Program," *Community Mental Health Journal*, 1967, *3*, 133–136. E. Phillips, "Parent-Child Psychotherapy: A Follow-up Study Comparing Two Techniques," *Journal of Psychology*, 1960, *49*, 195–202.

30. B. Guerney, ed., *Psychotherapeutic Agents: New Roles for Non-professionals, Parents, and Teachers*, Holt, Rinehart, and Winston, 1969. See also E. Gendlin and J. Rychlak, "Psychotherapeutic Processes," *Annual Review of Psychology*, 1970, *21*, 170–171. T. Scheff, "Reevaluation Counseling: Social Implications," *Journal of Humanistic Psychol.*, 1972, *12* (1), 58–71. R. Carkhuff and C. Truax, "Lay Mental Health Counseling: The Effects of Lay Group Counseling," *J. Consult. Psychol.*, 1965, *29*, 426–431. E. F. Linton, "The Nonprofessional Scene," *American Child*, 1967, *49* (1), 9–13. F. Sobey, *The Nonprofessional Revolution in Mental Health*, Columbia University Press, 1970; John W. Drakeford, *Farewell to the Lonely Crowd*, Word Books, 1969; Walter O'Connell, "Psychotherapy for Everyman," *Journal of Existentialism*, Fall 1966, *7* (25).

31. Pierre Teilhard de Chardin, *Hymn of the Universe*, Harper & Row, 1961, 75 ff; R. P. Garrigou-Lagrange, *La Philosophie de l'Etre et le Sens Commun*, Beauchesne, 1904; Buber, *BMM*, 15 ff.

32. John Henry Cardinal Newman, *An Essay in Aid of a Grammar of Assent*, Longmans, Green, 1903, chap 9. See also Herberg, *Martin Buber: Personalist Philosopher in an Age of Depersonalization*, St. Joseph College, 1972, 2 ff.

33. John Henry Cardinal Newman, *The Essential Newman*, ed. V. F. Blehl, New American Library, 1963, "Interpersonal Communication," 167 ff. W. L. La Croix, *Patterns, Values and Horizon: An Ethic*, Corpus, 1970.

II. THE GAME-FREE RELATIONSHIP

1. An early definition of intimacy as a "game-free relationship" may be found in Berne's *The Structure and Dynamics of Organizations and Groups*, Grove Press, 1963; cf. Thomas A. Harris, *I'm OK—You're OK*, Harper & Row, 1969, 124.

2. Berne, *SHL*, 114–116; Claude Steiner and Carmen Kerr, *TA Made Simple*, Ra Press, 1971, 7.

3. Berne, *TAP*. For the many who have already been introduced to TA, another introduction is hardly needed. In fact, one of the irritations of the TA

literature is that it contains such deadening repetitions. Virtually every TA discussion begins with a self-conscious introduction. Thus, if anyone wishes to get an elementary introduction, he should read the early chapters of Berne's *GPP, Hello,* or *TAP,* or Steiner or Harris.

4. TRANSACTIONAL ANALYSIS: ITS IMPLICIT FAITH

1. Berne, *TAP,* 29 ff.

2. Kenneth Everts, "TA and Pastoral Counseling," *TA Bulletin,* October 1966, 5, 173 f.; Richard E. Chartier, "A Plan for Getting TA into Church and Community," *TA Bulletin,* 1970, 8, 16; see "TA Study Group at Holy Cross Abbey," ibid., 18.

3. Kenneth N. Edelman, "Is Theology Adult?," *Transactional Analysis Journal,* January 1973, 3 (3), 50 ff.; Harris, "P-A-C and Religion," 226 ff.; cf. Clark, J.V. "Toward a Theory and Practice of Religious Experiences, in J. F. T. Bugental, ed., *Challenges of Humanistic Psychology,* McGraw-Hill, 1967.

4. For the structure I am indebted to Edward C. Hobbs, *motive,* May 1957, 28ff. Cf. Oden, *The Intensive Group Experience,* Westminster Press, 1972, 103 ff. (hereafter *IGE*); *KC,* chap. 3.

5. Harris, *I'm OK,* 27.

6. C. Steiner, *Games Alcoholics Play,* Grove Press, 1971, 6. (hereafter *GAP).*

7. Berne, *SHL,* 84.

8. Augustine, *On the Trinity,* 10:11, 17–18, in M. Dods, ed., *Works of Aurelius Augustinus,* T. & T. Clark, 1871 ff., Vol. 7.

9. Harris, *I'm OK,* 32.

10. Ibid., 33.

11. Ibid., 30.

12. Steiner, *GAP,* 8.

13. *Augustine: Later Works,* ed. John Burnaby, SCM, 1955, LCC VIII, "The Trinity," 89.

14. Steiner, *GAP,* 12.

15. L. I. Newman, ed., *The Hasidic Anthology,* Bloch, 1944, 389.

16. Harris, *I'm OK,* 41.

17. Berne., *Hello,* 123.

18. Penfield, "Memory Mechanisms," *A.M.A. Archives of Neurology and Psychiatry,*67, 1952, 178 ff.

19. Harris, *I'm OK,* 11.

20. Augustine, in *Fathers of the Church,* ed. R. Deferrari et al., Fathers of the Church, 1948 ff, "Confessions", 10:13.

21. Penfield, op. cit., 178 ff.
22. Harris, *I'm OK*, 37.
23. Ibid., 27.
24. James and Jongeward, *BW*, 35.
25. Berne, *Hello*, 85.
26. Ibid., 446.
27. Ibid., 32.
28. Ibid.
29. Ibid., 53.
30. Calvin, *Institutes of the Christian Religion*, trans. J. Allen, Presbyterian Church USA, 1936, 2 vols., Book 2 chaps. 1, 7.
31. Berne, *Hello*, 71.
32. E. W. Plass, ed., *What Luther Says*, Concordia Publishing House, 1959 (hereafter *WLS*), 1:138.
33. Berne, *Hello*, 444.
34. Ibid., 204.
35. Ibid., 275.
36. Justin Martyr, *First Apology, Early Christian Fathers*, ed. C. C. Richardson, Westminster Press, 1953, LCC I, 249 ff.
37. Berne, *Hello*, 443.
38. Ibid., 110.
39. Ibid., 275.
40. Ibid., 118.
41. *WLS*, 1:400.
42. Berne, *Hello*, 115.
43. *WLS*, 1:395.
47. Berne, *Hello*, 122.
45. Tertullian, "On Penitence," in W. A. Clebsch and C. R. Jaekle, eds., *Pastoral Care in Historical Perspective*, Prentice-Hall, 1964, 97.
46. Berne, *Hello*, 443.
47. *WLS*, 1:394.
48. Berne, *Hello*, 23.
49. Ibid.
50. Ibid.
51. Ibid.
52. Steiner, *GAP*, 13.
53. Berne, *Hello*, 210.
54. Steiner, *GAP*, 16.
55. The Baal Shem Tov. in L. I. Newman, ed., *The Hasidic Anthology* (hereafter *HA*), Bloch, 1944, 432–433.

56. James and Jongeward, *BW*, 30.

57. Ibid.

58. Calvin, *Institutes*, II, i, 9.

59. Berne, *Hello*, 123 ff, 374–376.

60. Karl Barth, *Church Dogmatics*, T. & T. Clark, 1931 ff., II/2, IV/2; Oden, *The Promise of Barth*, Lippincott, 1969, 65 ff.

61. Berne, *Hello*, 124; cf. Steiner, "TA as a Treatment Philosophy," *TA Bulletin*, July 1968, 7 (27), 61 ff.

62. Oden, *KC*, chap. 2.

63. A. T. van Leeuwen, " 'Christianization' and Secularization," *Christianity in World History*, Scribner's, 1964, 411 ff.; Larry Shiner, *The Secularization of History*, Abingdon Press, 1966.

64. Claude M. Steiner and Ursula Steiner, "Permission Classes," *Transactional Analysis Bulletin* 1968, 7 (28), 89.

65. For a discussion of the limits of such analogies, see my previous study of analogy, *KC*, chap. 4.

66. Berne, *Hello*, 144.

67. *HA*, 380.

68. Berne, *Hello*, 153.

69. Ibid., 53.

70. The Bratzlaver Rabbi, *HA*, 391.

71. Berne, *Hello*, 144.

72. The Riziner Rabbi, *HA*, 433.

73. Berne, *Hello*, 143.

74. Tertullian, "On Penitence", Clebsch and Jaekle, *Pastoral Care*, 98.

75. Berne, *Hello*, 124.

76. Pat Crossman, *TA Bulletin*, July 1966, 5 (19), 152.

77. Steiner, *GAP*, 160.

78. *TA Bulletin*, January 1968, 7 (25) 2.

79. Epistle of Barnabas, *The Apostolic Fathers*, trans. K. Lake, W. Heinemann, 1913, Loeb Classical Library, 1:409.

80. Steiner, *TA Bulletin*, April 1966, 15 (18), 135.

81. *St. Thomas Aquinas*, ed. T. Gilby, Oxford University Press, 1955, 187 (hereafter *STA*).

82. Berne, *Hello*, 127.

83. Ibid., 123.

84. Ibid., 127.

85. H. T. Kerr, ed., *Readings in Christian Thought*, Abingdon, 1966, 115 (hereafter *RCT*).

86. Steiner, *GAP*, 143.

87. Ibid., 8.
88. Berne, *Hello,* 6.
89. Harris, *I'm OK,* 50 f.
90. Berne, *Hello.*
91. *HA,* 380.
92. Claude Steiner and Ursula Steiner, "Permission Groups," *TA Bulletin,* October 1968, *7* (28), 89.
93. *RCT,* 195.
94. *TA Bulletin,* July 1966, 5 (17), 154.
95. Harris, *I'm OK,* 43.
96. *STA,* 119.
97. Steiner, *GAP,* xvii.
98. *RCT,* 23.
99. Berne, *Hello,* 276.
100. *WLS,* 1:393.
101. Harris, *I'm OK,* 50.
102. Pascal, *Pensées,* Penguin, 1966, 150.
103. Berne, *Hello,* 25.
104. Ibid., 143.
105. Second Epistle of Clement, in Clebsch and Jaekle, *Pastoral Care,* 90.
106. Berne, *Hello,* 266.
107. James and Jongeward, *BW,* 59.
108. Berne, *SHL,* 234.
109. Rabbi Hillel, Avoth 1:14, quoted by Buber, *I and Thou,* 85n.
110. James and Jongeward, *BW,* 58.
111. Baal Shem Tov, in Buber, *Hasidism and Modern Man,* Harper & Row, 1966, 191.
112. Berne, *Hello,* 88.
113. James and Jongeward, *BW,* 58.
114. Tertullian, *The Apology,* Ante-Nicene Christian Library, T. & T. Clark, 1895, 11:123.
115. Berne, *Hello,* 276.
116. Kenneth Everts, *TA Bulletin,* October 1966, 5 (20), 173.
117. *RCT,* 204.
118. Berne, *Hello,* 1.
119. Ibid., 3, 4.
120. *HA,* 219.

5. A LETTER TO FROGS AND PRINCES

1. The verse numbers in this section correspond generally with the traditional verse numbering of Paul's letter to the Romans.

6. WHO SAYS YOU'RE OK?—
A CRITIQUE OF TRANSACTIONAL ANALYSIS

1. Berne, "Classification of Positions," *TA Bulletin*, July 1962, *1* (23).
2. Berne, *Hello*, 86.
3. Ibid., 90–91.
4. Ibid., 89; James and Jongeward, *BW*, 34.
5. Berne, *Principles of Group Treatment*, Grove Press, 1966, 270.
6. Harris, *I'm OK*, chaps. 3, 4; Berne, "Classification of Positions."
7. Steiner and Kerr, *TA Made Simple*, 4–6; Steiner, *GAP*, Part 2.
8. Exodus 1–20; Hosea 1:1 ff.; 2 Cor. 5:14–20.
9. H. R. Mackintosh, *The Christian Experience of Forgiveness*, Collins Fontana Books, 1961.
10. John 2:13–17; 2 Samuel 12:1–13; Amos 2:6–4:13; Jeremiah 2:1 ff.
11. Luther, *Works*, Muhlenberg Press, 1943, 2:301 ff.
12. Berne, *Hello*, 97 ff., 122 ff., 445; cf. Steiner and Kerr, *TA Made Simple*, 4.
13. A. Daigon and R. LaConte, *Dig U.S.A.*, Bantam, 1970; H. G. Ginott, *Between Parent and Child*, Macmillan, 1965.
14. Berne, *Hello*, Part 2; Thomas L. Shaffer, "The Law and Order Game," *TA Bulletin*, 1970, *8*, 41 ff.
15. Berne, *TAP*, 240; *Hello*, 445.
16. Berne, *Hello*, 104–105; *GPP*, 26.
17. Berne, *Hello*, 104–105; *TAP*, 117; J. D. White, "Adapted Child Complexes," *TA Bulletin*, 1970, *8*, 150 ff.
18. "Eric Berne said people are born princes and princesses and their parents turn them into frogs. What this means is that TA therapists see people as basically OK and in difficulty only because their parents have placed damaging injunctions on them." Steiner and Kerr, *TA Made Simple*, 1971, 15.
19. E. Bergler, Liveright, 1964.
20. Exodus 20:12.
21. See Richard La Piere, *The Freudian Ethic*, Allen and Unwin, 1960.
22. A similar point has been made by Midge Dechter, *The New Chastity and Other Arguments Against Women's Liberation*, Coward, McCann and Geoghegan, 1972.

23. For a partial corrective see William Glasser, *Reality Therapy,* Harper & Row, 1965; Perry London, *The Modes and Morals of Psychotherapy,* Holt, Rinehart, and Winston, 1964; Erik H. Erikson, *Childhood and Society,* Norton, 1950; "Identity and the Life Cycle," *Psychological Issues,* 1959, *1* (1).

24. Berne, *GPP,* 15–20; *PGT,* 230–232; Harris, *I'm OK,* chap. 7; Steiner, *GAP,* 122 ff.; Ira J. Tanner, Loneliness, 81 ff.

25. Berne, *SHL,* 144ff.; Harris, *I'm OK,* 123–125.

26. S. P. Spitzer, ed., *The Sociology of Personality,* Van Nostrand–Reinhold, 1969; M. S. Olmsted, *The Small Group,* Random House, 1959; P. Berger, *The Precarious Vision,* Doubleday, 1961; H. H. Gerth and C. W. Mills, eds., *From Max Weber,* Oxford University Press, 1958; E. P. Hollander and R. G. Hunt, eds., *Current Perspectives in Social Psychology,* Oxford University Press, 1963.

27. Berne, *SHL,* passim; cf. Max Weber, *The Protestant Ethic and the Spirit of Capitalism,* Scribner's, 1930.

28. E. Berne, "History of the ITAA—1958–1968," *TA Bulletin,* January 1968, 7 (25), 19 f.

29. Berne, *Hello,* 117.

30. Ibid., 37.

31. Ibid., 119.

32. *TA Bulletin,* 9 (33), 57.

33. Berne, *Hello,* 176–182.

34. Ibid., 23.

35. Berne, *GPP;* Edgar C. Stuntz, *Transactional Game Analysis: A Review of TA Literature 1962 through 1970,* Transactional Pubs., 1970; cf. Robert Zechnich, "Good Games," *Transactional Analysis Journal,* January 1973, *3* (3).

36. Berne, *Hello,* 89 f.; 203–205; Harris, *I'm OK;* Steiner, *GAP,* 33 ff.; James and Jongeward, *BW,* 1–6. Dorothy Jongeward and Muriel James, *Winning with People: Group Exercises in Transactional Analysis,* Addison-Wesley, 1973.

37. V. Frankl, *Man's Search for Meaning,* Beacon Press, 1963.

38. 2 Corinthians 12:1–10.

39. O. H. Mowrer, *The Crisis in Psychiatry and Religion,* Van Nostrand, 1961; *The New Group Therapy,* Van Nostrand, 1964; *Learning Theory and Behavior,* Wiley, 1960; O. H. Mowrer, ed., *Morality and Mental Health,* Rand McNally, 1967.

40. For further perceptive discussions of this point see Clemens E. Benda, *Gewissen und Schuld: Die Psychiatrische, Religiöse und Politische Interpretation des Schuldig-seins,* F. K. Schattauer Verlag, 1970; John G. McKenzie, *Guilt: Its Meaning and Significance,* Cokesbury, 1966; Wilfred L. LaCroix, *Patterns,*

Values and Horizon: An Ethic, Corpus Books, 1970; "Moral Value and Interpersonal Relations," 81 ff.; cf. Oden, *SA*, Part 2.

41. Berne, *Hello*, chap. 19; cf. Muzafer Sherif, "Group Influences upon the Formation of Norms and Attitudes," *Readings in Social Psychology*, Maccoby, Newcomb, and Hartley. Holt, Rinehart & Winston, 1958.

42. Karl Barth, *Church Dogmatics*, III/4, T. & T. Clark, 1961, 116 ff.; Helmut Thielicke, *Theological Ethics*, Vol. 1, ed. W. Lazareth, Fortress Press, 1966; Oden, *Radical Obedience*, Westminster Press, 1964, chap. 4.

43. Berne, *Hello*, 446; see also "Giving Up My Old Parent and Incorporating a New Parent, Patients' Autobiographies," *TA Bulletin*, July 1969, 8 (31), 68 ff.; "Outpatient Reparenting," *TA Bulletin*, 1970, *8*, 135 f.; J. L. Schiff, *TA Bulletin*, July 1969, 8 (31), 47 ff.

44. Jean Piaget, *The Moral Judgment of the Child*, Harcourt, Brace, 1932; C. Ellis Nelson, ed., *Conscience: Theological and Psychological Perspectives*, Newman Press, 1973.

45. Berne, *Hello*, chap. 15.

46. A. Cohen, *Everyman's Talmud*, Dutton, 1949, chaps. 3, 6, 10; G. F. Moore, *Judaism in the First Centuries of the Christian Era*, Harvard University Press, 1927–30, Vol. 2.

47. Thomas Hobbes, *Leviathan*, ed. M. Oakeshott, Barnes & Noble, 1966.

48. Basil Willey, *The English Moralists*, Norton, 1964.

49. Vernon Bourke, *History of Ethics*, Doubleday, 1968, chap. 8. F. Copleston, *History of Philosophy*, Doubleday, 1962, Vol. 1.

50. Berne, *Hello*, 12.

III. A THEOLOGY OF PERSONAL TRANSACTIONS

1. The term "encounter culture" refers to a recognizable subculture that has emerged in and around the human potential movement and human relations training groups, including T-groups, Gestalt groups, TA groups, basic encounter groups, growth groups, etc., with their growth centers, sensory awareness exercises, therapeutic stratagems and encounter life-style. Sociologically, the subculture may be said to exhibit its own norms, mores, language, and artifacts. It has its own saints, authority structures, pilgrimages, and hallowed forms of traditioning. For a more detailed definition of the "encounter culture," see my introduction to *IGE*, 17–27. Among the representative studies that illustrate basic directions of the subculture, see Carl Rogers, *Carl Rogers on Encounter Groups*, Harper & Row, 1970; Arthur Burton, ed., *Encounter*, Jossey-Bass, 1969; C. R. Mill, *Selections from Human Relations Training News*, National Training Laboratories, 1969; Warren G. Bennis et al., eds., *The Planning of Change*, 2nd

ed., Holt, Rinehart, and Winston, 1969; Howard R. Lewis and Harold S. Streitfeld, *Growth Games*, Harcourt Brace Jovanovich, 1971; William Schutz, *Joy;* Bernard Gunther, *Sense Relaxation: Below Your Mind*, Collier Books, 1968; Daniel I. Malamud and Solomon Machover, *Toward Self-Understanding: Group Techniques in Self-Confrontation*, Charles C. Thomas, 1965; Sam Keen, "The Soft Revolution," *The Christian Century*, December 31, 1967, 1667; Herbert A. Otto, ed., *Human Potentialities: The Challenge and the Promise*, Warren H. Green, 1968; Jane Howard, *Please Touch*, McGraw-Hill, 1970.

2. Among earlier attempts to understand the religious dimensions of intensive group experiencing are the following: John L. Casteel, ed., *Spiritual Renewal Through Personal Groups*, Association Press, 1957; Ross Snyder, "Group Dynamics in the Life of the Church," *Religious Education*, November 1951; Harold W. Freer and F. B. Hall, *Two or Three Together*, Harper & Bros., 1954. For more recent discussions, see William W. Meisner, *Group Dynamics in the Religious Life*, University of Notre Dame Press, 1965; Clyde Reid, *Groups Alive—Church Alive*, Harper & Row, 1969; Robert C. Leslie, *Sharing Groups in the Church*, Abingdon Press, 1970; James V. Clark, "Toward a Theory and Practice of Religious Experiencing," in J. F. T. Bugental, ed., *The Challenge for Humanistic Psychology*, McGraw-Hill, 1966; Sam Keen, *To a Dancing God*, Harper & Row, 1970.

7. THE TASK OF TRANSACTIONAL THEOLOGY

1. Søren Kierkegaard, *Stages along Life's Way*, Princeton University Press, 1945.

2. A. Nygren, *Agape and Eros*, SPCK, 1953.

3. Timothy Leary, *Interpersonal Diagnosis of Personality*, Ronald Press, 1957; Erving Goffman, *Encounters*, Bobbs-Merrill, 1961; *Strategic Interaction*, University of Pennsylvania Press, 1969; H. S. Sullivan, *The Interpersonal Theory of Psychiatry* W. W. Norton, 1953; Patrick Mullahy, ed., *The Contributions of Harry Stack Sullivan*, Hermitage House, 1952; William C. Schutz, *FIRO: A Three-Dimensional Theory of Interpersonal Behavior*, Rinehart & Company, 1958; E. Shostrom, *Man the Manipulator*, Abingdon, 1967; J. W. Thibaut and H. H. Kelley, *The Social Psychology of Groups*, Wiley, 1959; Robert F. Bales, *Interaction Process Analysis*, Addison-Wesley, 1951. See also L. Festinger, *A Theory of Cognitive Dissonance*, Stanford University Press, 1957; J. W. Brehm, A. R. Cohen, *Explorations in Cognitive Dissonance*, Wiley, 1962; Kurt Lewin, *Resolving Social Conflicts*, Harper & Bros., 1948; Alfred Schutz, *Collected Papers*, 2 vols., ed. A. Brodersen, Martinus Nijhoff, 1962; G. C. Homans, *Social Behavior*, Harcourt, Brace, 1961.

4. R. D. Laing, H. Phillipson, A. R. Lee, *Interpersonal Perception: A Theory and a Method of Research*, Harper & Row, 1966, F. Heider, *The Psychology of Interpersonal Relations*, Wiley, 1958.

5. "The New Pietism," *Journal of Humanistic Psychology*, Winter 1972; *IGE*, chap 2.

6. Originally projected as a part of this study, but later omitted, was a detailed exegetical-theological study of "Jesus' Transactional Style," focusing on the hypothesis that the deepest clues to Jesus' understanding of his mission are revealed in his specific remembered encounters with persons in his environment: opponents, followers, family, close friends, the establishment, outcasts, prostitutes, tax collectors, etc. That study, which will be published separately, may be considered as the part of the original design of this study that was intended to function as the biblical-exegetical support for this theological argument. In its absence my discussion admittedly lacks a certain exegetical specificity. In time, however, this will be available to readers who wish to pursue the biblical-exegetical dimensions of our theme.

7. Martin Buber, *BMM*; Maurice S. Friedman, *Martin Buber*, University of Chicago, 1955; Paul Tournier, *The Whole Person in a Broken World*, Harper & Row, 1964; *To Understand Each Other*, John Knox Press, 1967; *The Meaning of Gifts*, John Knox Press, 1961; *The Meaning of Persons*, Harper & Row, 1957; *The Healing of Persons*, Harper & Row, 1965; *The Person Reborn*, Harper & Row, 1966; Marc Oraison, *Being Together*, 1970; H. R. Niebuhr, *The Meaning of Revelation*, Macmillan, 1962; cf. R. R. Niebuhr, *Experiential Religion*, Harper & Row, 1972; Frank Lake, *Clinical Theology: A Theological and Psychiatric Basis to Clinical Pastoral Care*, Darton Longman & Todd, 1966. See also Emil Brunner, *Truth as Encounter*, trans. A. W. Loos and D. Cairns, Westminster Press, 1964; *Man in Revolt: A Christian Anthropology*, Westminster Press, 1947, 278 ff.; Nicolas Berdyaev, *Solitude and Society*, Geoffrey Bles 1958; *Slavery and Freedom*, Scribner's, 1944; *Destiny of Man*, Geoffrey Bles, 1937; *The Fate of Man in the Modern World*, University of Michigan Press, 1961; Daniel Day Williams, *The Spirit and the Forms of Love*, Harper & Row, 1968; Reuel L. Howe, *The Miracle of Dialogue*, Seabury Press, 1963; Frederick Greeves, *Theology and the Cure of Souls: An Introduction to Pastoral Theology*, Epworth Press, 1960, 99 ff.; Carlyle Marney, *The Recovery of the Person: A Christian Humanism*, Abingdon Press, 1963.

8. Augustine, *The Confessions*, trans. Dods, Modern Library, 1949; John T. McNeill, *A History of the Cure of Souls*, Harper & Bros., 1951; Karl Barth, *Church Dogmatics*, Vol. 4, Part 2, T. & T. Clark, 1958, 727 ff.; Louis Bouyer, *Introduction to Spirituality*, Desclee, 1961; Anne Fremantle, ed., *The Protestant Mystics*, Weidenfeld and Nicolson, 1964.

9. Quoted by Jacques Maritain, *The Person and the Common Good*, University of Notre Dame Press, 1966, 20, (PCG).

10. Will Herberg first called my attention to this. See his *Martin Buber: Personalist Philosopher in an Age of Depersonalization*, McAuley Lecture 15, St. Joseph College, 1972.

11. Buber, *I and Thou;* Ferdinand Ebner, *Das Wort und die geistigen Realitäten*, Regensburg, 1921; Maritain (PCG), Berdyaev, *Solitude and Society, op cit.;* Friedrich Gogarten, *Von Glauben und Offenbarung*, Eugen Diederichs, 1923. For further development of this thesis see Jacob L. Moreno, "The Viennese Origins of the Encounter Movement, Paving the Way for Existentialism, Group Psychotherapy and Psychodrama," *Group Psychotherapy*, 1969, *22*, 7–16; Moreno, *Einladung zu einer Begegnung*, Anzengruber, 1914; *Rede über den Augenblick*, Kiepenheuer, 1922; Karl Barth, *Der Römerbrief* (1919 Auflage), EVZ-Verlag, 1963; Emmanuel Mounier, *Personalism*, trans. P. Mariet, University of Notre Dame Press, 1970; G. H. Mead, *Mind, Self, and Society*, University of Chicago Press, 1934.

12. Augustine, *City of God*, trans. Dods, Modern Library, 1950 (hereafter *CG*), J. N. D. Kelly, *Early Christian Creeds*, Longmans, 1950; Emil Brunner, *The Divine Imperative*, trans. O. Wyon, Westminster Press, 1937, 293 ff.

13. Maritain, *Person and the Common Good*, 23.

14. Augustine, *CG*, 692.

15. St. Thomas Aquinas, *Summa Theologiae* (Blackfriars), Vol. 46, McGraw-Hill, 1966.

16. Jacob Needleman, *The New Religions*, Pocket Books, 1970; Meher Baba, *Listen Humanity*, Dodd, Mead, 1967; Maharishi Mahesh Yogi, *The Science of Being and the Art of Living*, Signet, 1963; Carlos Castaneda, *A Separate Reality*, Simon and Schuster, 1971.

17. I am referring to authors indicated in notes 7 and 11 above.

18. For a persuasive defense of all these conditions see W. Pannenberg, *BQT.*

19. See note 3 above. Robert Carson, *Interaction Concepts of Personality*, Aldine, 1969, is the best review of this literature.

20. See N. Hartmann, *Ethics*, Vol. 2, Macmillan, 1932.

21. Pannenberg, *BQT*, 2:212 ff.; K. Barth, *Evangelical Theology: An Introduction*, Holt, Rinehart & Winston, 1963.

22. Saint Anselm, *Basic Writings*, trans. S. N. Deane, Open Court, 1966, 172 ff.; George H. Williams, *Anselm: Communion and Atonement*, Concordia, 1959; Karl Barth, *Anselm: Fides Quaerens Intellectum*, Meridian Books, 1962; Don S. Browning, *Atonement and Psychotherapy*, Westminster Press, 1966, 51 ff.

23. Analogy is subject to abuse in its every use. For a methodological study of the responsible use of analogy, see my discussion in *Kerygma and Counseling*, chap. 4.

24. *SA*, 15 ff., 232 ff.

25. Paul Henry, *Saint Augustine on Personality*, Macmillan, 1960, argues that the notion of personhood requires a trinitarian structure.

26. John H. Leith, ed., *Creeds of the Churches*, Doubleday, 1963, 28 ff; Reinhold Seeberg, *Textbook of the History of Doctrines*, Baker Book House, 1952.

27. "The Definition of Chalcedon," John Leith ed., *Creeds of the Churches*, 36.

8. TOWARD A REALISTIC INTERPERSONALISM

1. The ensuing analysis is indebted in particular to the works of Søren Kierkegaard and Reinhold Niebuhr, esp. Kierkegaard, *The Concept of Dread*, trans. W. Lowrie, Princeton University Press, 1946; *Fear and Trembling and Sickness unto Death*, trans. W. Lowrie, Doubleday, 1954 (hereafter *FTSD*); R. Niebuhr, *The Nature and Destiny of Man*, 2 vols., Scribner's, 1948 (hereafter *NDM*); *The Self and the Dramas of History*, Scribner's, 1953 *(SDH)*; *Love and Justice*, ed. D. B. Robertson, Westminster Press, 1957 *(LJ)*; also John Oman, *Grace and Personality*, Cambridge University Press, 1917.

2. Brunner, *Man in Revolt*, 114 ff.; see also R. D. Laing, "Ontological Insecurity," in H. M. Rutenbeck, ed., *Psychoanalysis and Existential Philosophy*, Dutton, 1962.

3. Desmond Morris, *The Naked Ape*, Dell, 1967; Robert Ardrey, *The Territorial Imperative*, Delta Books, 1966; cf. H. F. Harlow, "Affectional Responses in Infant Monkeys," *Science*, 1959 *130*; J. N. Bleibtreu, *The Parable of the Beast*, Collier, 1968; S. J. Dimond, *The Social Behavior of Animals*, Harper & Row, 1970.

4. C. E. Sheedy, *The Christian Virtues*, University of Notre Dame Press, 1949.

5. Kierkegaard, *FTSD*, 166 ff.

6. Ibid., 163 ff.

7. R. Niebuhr, *NDM*, 1:241 ff.

8. Ibid., 260.

9. Leary, Thibaut, and Kelley, Carson, as cited earlier; see also U. G. Foa, "Convergences in the Analysis of the Structures of Interpersonal Behavior," *Psychological Review*, 1961, *69*, 341–53.

10. Paul Tillich, *Love, Power and Justice*, Oxford University Press, 1954.

11. Carson, *Interaction Concepts*, chap. 5.

12. T. Minnema, *The Social Ethics of Reinhold Niebuhr: A Structural Analysis*, J. H. Kok N. V. Kampen, 1958.

13. Reinhold Niebuhr, *NDM*, 2, chap. 11, and *Faith and History*, Scribner's, 1949.

14. R. Niebuhr, *LJ;* Paul Ramsey, *Basic Christian Ethics*, SCM, 1953, chap. 9.

15. R. Niebuhr, *An Interpretation of Christian Ethics*, Harper & Brothers, 1935; *LJ*, Part 1.

EPILOGUE

1. J. F. T. Bugental, *The Search for Authenticity*, Holt, Rinehart, & Winston, 1965.

2. G. Egan, *Encounter: Group Processes for Interpersonal Growth*, Brooks/-Cole, 1970; William C. Schutz, *Here Comes Everybody; Body-Mind and Encounter Culture*, Harper & Row, 1971; A. Burton, ed., *Encounter: Theory and Practices of Encounter Groups*, Jossey-Bass, 1969.

3. M. Cahn, "Where Goes the T-Group When It's Over?," *Human Relations Training News*, 1969, *13* (4), 6–7.

4. A. W. Watts, *The Joyous Cosmology: Adventures in the Chemistry of Consciousness*, Random House, 1962; John White, ed., *The Highest State of Consciousness*, Doubleday, 1972, esp. W. N. Pahnke, "Drugs to Mysticism," 257 ff.

5. Rasa Gustaitis, *Turning On*, New American Library, 1969.

6. Theodore Roszak, *Where the Wasteland Ends*, Doubleday, 1973.

7. Herbert Marcuse, *One Dimensional Man*, Beacon Press, 1966; Kenneth Keniston, *The Uncommitted: Alienated Youth in American Society*, Dell, 1967; Theodore Roszak, *The Making of a Counter Culture*, Doubleday, 1969; Charles Reich, *The Greening of America*, Random House, 1970.

8. *Future Shock*, Bantam Books, 1970.

9. *The Republic*, trans. F. M. Cornford, Oxford University Press, 1956.

10. Peter Blau, *Exchange and Power in Social Life*, Wiley, 1964; Michael Argyle, *The Psychology of Interpersonal Behavior*, Penguin Books, 1967; George C. Homans, *The Human Group*, Harcourt, Brace, 1950; *Social Behavior: Its Elementary Forms*.

11. Karl Barth, *Church Dogmatics*, II/2, T. & T. Clark, 1957.

Subject Index

Acceptance, 6f., 48, 82ff.
Accountability, 13, 26, 35f.
Adam, 54, 76
Adapted Child, 78ff., 88
Adolescent psychotherapy, 88
Adult ego-state, 47ff., 73ff.
Affection, 3, 17f.
Agape, 85, 128
Alienation, 48ff., 123ff., 133–135
Analogy, 34ff., 48ff., 62, 110, 116, 127, 154
Anorgasmophobia, 32
Anxiety, 26ff., 123ff.
Atonement, 114ff.
Aura perceptions, 21
Authenticity, 13ff., 130ff.
Autonomy, 20, 61, 77
Availability, 7
Awareness, 85
Awe, 9

Behavioral Psychology, 20
Beholding, 3, 8, 18, 138
Bible, 3, 7, 12, 47ff., 81, 88, 135
Blockages, 7, 27, 49
Body, 121ff.

Body language, 21, 23, 62, 77
Bonding, 14

Care, caring, 4, 53, 70
Case study method, 105
Chalcedon, Council of, 118
Child ego-state, 47ff., 78ff.
  adapted, 78ff., 88
  natural, 78ff., 88
Christ event, 60ff., 106, 110, 114ff., 128f.
Christian hope, 22
Christian social philosophy, 108
Christology, 114–119
Closeness, 6ff., 19
Collusion, 79f., 104, 125
Commitment, 5, 8, 13
Communication, 21, 109
Communion, interpersonal, 43, 99ff.
Confession, 49ff., 86, 94–96
Conflict-capability, 5, 12, 17ff., 35
Congruence, 7, 14, 17, 34ff.
Conscience, 95f.
Contractual clarity, 13f., 23f., 34ff., 126
Control, 9, 21, 27
Conversion, 66
Covenant fidelity, 13, 42f., 81, 114f.

Death, 16f., 21, 29, 77, 121
Decision, 67f.
Deliverance, 48ff., 60, 80f.
Demon, demonic, 57f., 78f., 124, 134
Devil, 58, 124
Dialectic, 26ff.
Distance, 21, 27
Doxology, 113, 121
Drug abuse, 131
Duration, 11ff.
Dyadic interaction, 104

Ecstasy, 8, 11, 32
Ego-state (*see also* Adult; Child; Parent),
    47ff., 87ff., 94ff.
Emotive warmth, 17, 21
Empathy, 12–16, 34ff.
Empiricism, 22, 121ff.
Encounter culture, 99ff., 130ff., 150
Esalen, 41, 135
Eternal, the, 10ff., 13, 22, 121ff.
Ethics, 81, 84, 90f., 111f.
Evangelical thought, 60ff., 72ff., 106
Explicit revelation, 85f.

Faithfulness, 42, 135
Fantasy, 5ff., 137
Finitude, 16, 21, 42, 121ff.
Forgiveness, 48, 60f., 85f., 135
Freedom, 7f., 65f., 74, 78, 121ff., 125
Friendship, 19, 27, 41f.
Future, 23

Gallows laugh, 56
Game, 20, 29, 58ff., 74, 89ff., 93, 131
Game-free relationship (*see also* Intimacy),
    18, 20, 45ff., 66ff.
Gestalt, 10, 103
Gift, 9
God, Christian understanding of, 16–18,
    41f., 48ff., 62, 72ff., 107ff., 134ff.
    enjoyment of, 108
    grace of, 62, 64ff., 86, 134
    the OK of, 72ff.
    personal, 107

revelation of, 109–114
    triune, 118
Grace, 62, 64ff., 86, 134
Greek philosophy, 97
Grief, 29
Ground of acceptance, 85
Group Assessment of Interpersonal Traits
    (GAIT), 42
Group processes, 60ff., 90, 99ff., 130ff.
Guilt, 55, 88, 94ff.
    real, 94f.

Hasidism, 63, 105
Hebraic understanding, 12f., 20, 33, 54,
    105, 131
Hell, 17, 32, 61, 73
Henosis, 7, 66
History, 10, 12, 23, 76, 85, 91, 110, 113,
    121
Honesty, 7, 20ff., 130ff.
Hope, 14
Hostility, 18
Hubris, 96, 123ff.
Human potential movement, 54, 130ff.

Idealism, 120ff., 126
Idol, idolatry, 22, 30
Implicit faith, 46ff., 82ff.
Incarnation, 16f., 61
Individual, individuation, 4, 14, 21, 28,
    108, 120ff.
Innigheit, 3
Interdisciplinary inquiry, 109–114
Intergenerational scripting, 54, 88
Interpersonal, sphere of the, 1ff., 6ff., 21,
    42ff., 123ff.
    communion, 21, 42ff., 102
    theology, 99ff.
Interpersonalism, 97, 106ff., 120ff.
Intimacy, ixff., 2–25, 65ff., 89ff.
    definition of, 2–25
    dilemmas of, 26ff.
    fantasy of, 5, 137f.
    fulfilling, 5, 137
    hazards of, 26ff.

hunger for, 2ff., 130ff.
language of, 2ff.
moments of, 5ff.
of things, of persons, 4
outward, 4
sexuality and, 31ff.
structured, 41f.
surrogate, 34
tactile, 19
types of, 5
Intimus sphere, 3ff., 12, 16, 30, 35, 117f.
Irony, 10ff.
Isolation, 28, 95

Jeder (Everyman), 54, 76
Judeo-Christian tradition, 23, 42f., 48ff.,
85ff., 99, 103, 120ff., 134
Justice, 127ff.

Laity, 62, 98
Language, 2ff., 43f., 51ff., 75, 91ff., 110ff.,
114–119, 121
Law, 64, 81, 112f., 114f.
Lay therapeutic agency, 39ff.
Letting-be, 9, 20
Limitation, 14, 121ff.
Love, 7, 36, 66ff., 85f., 108, 128ff., 135

Manipulation, 20, 32, 132
Meaning, 8, 30, 99ff.
Meditation, 5, 51, 108
Memory, 13, 51f., 135
Modernity, 43
Moments of intimacy, 6ff., 13
Mystery, 6, 9f., 42f., 86, 118, 124

National Training Laboratories, 102ff.
Natural Child, 78ff., 88
Nonpossessive warmth, 34ff.
Nonverbal communication, 21
Not OK Position, 54ff., 74, 81

OK Position, 48, 72ff., 82ff.
Ontology of acceptance, 82ff.

Orthodoxy, Christian, 18, 53
Outward intimacy, 4

Paradox, 10ff., 113, 120ff.
Parasensory, 21, 23
Parent ego-state, 47ff., 75, 80, 87ff.,
94ff.
nurturing, 80, 87
pig, 87ff.
prejudicial, 87ff.
Permission, 60ff., 81, 92
Person, 108, 117ff.
Personalism, 107–109
Personhood, 120ff.
Phenomenology, 5, 111
Pietism, 105, 134
Political ethics, 90f., 127
Populism, 38, 98
Positions, OK and not OK, 48, 54ff., 72ff.,
81ff.
Power, interpersonal, 125ff.
Predicament, human, 48ff., 73f.
Presence, 7, 43
Pride, 123, 127
Professionalization, therapeutic, 40ff.
Programming, 53
Protestant work ethic, 90f.
Psychology, 111
Psychotherapy, 34ff.
as surrogate intimacy, 34ff.
average, 36ff., 90
professional, 40ff.

Rabbinic tradition, 53ff., 96
Realism, 120ff.
Reality orientation, 83
Reason, 47ff., 73ff., 79, 97, 112, 126
Religious thought, western 42ff., 87, 101
contemporary, 101, 116
Re-Parenting, 62, 94, 97
Repentance, 63
Restitution, 95
Resurrection, 23, 67, 76ff., 86, 94
Revelation, 109–114
Ritual transaction, 89f.

Sacrificial love, 85, 128f.
Salvation, 31, 60ff.
Scripts, analysis of, 47ff., 53ff., 71ff.
  hamartic, 80
Security operations, 19, 29, 121ff.
Self-awareness, 6, 15, 17
Self-disclosure, 3, 20f., 85f.
Self-transcendence, 22, 120ff.
Sensuality, 123, 127
Sex, sexuality, 29, 31ff., 59, 66ff., 73
  and intimacy, 2f., 5, 31ff.
Sharing, 8ff., 15
Sin, 54ff., 123ff., 134
Social cohesion, 87f.
Sociology, interpersonal, 112, 133, 150
Solitude, 11, 28, 108
Soteriology, 60ff.
Spirit, 22f., 62, 121ff.
Spontaneity, 6
Spontaneous remission rate, 36
Stroking, 18, 28, 46, 53
Surrogate intimacy, 34ff.
Sweatshirt mottoes, 92f.
Symbiosis, 15

Talmud, 97
Temptation, 58f., 123f.
Termination, contractual, 13ff., 36
Theology, 16f., 18, 48ff., 99ff., 109ff.
Theology of Personal Transactions, 102ff.
Therapeutic triad, 38ff.
Therapy, 34ff.

Time, 10ff., 13, 28, 131
Touch, 19
Trading Stamps, 59, 63ff.
Transaction, 44ff., 99ff., 105, 114–119
  Christ event as, 106, 114ff.
  etymology of, 114f.
  theology of personal, 102ff.
Transactional Analysis, 18, 20, 41, 45ff.,
    71ff., 82ff., 103
  critique of, 82ff.
  beyond, x, 82ff.
Transcendence, 22, 121ff.
Transference, 35
Transpersonal, 6, 9ff., 42ff.
Trust, 6f., 75
Truth-telling, 20

Unconditional positive regard, 18f., 34ff.
Understanding, 16
Utilitarianism, 127

Value, 29, 90f., 111, 123

Warmth, 17ff.
Western religious consciousness, 42ff.,
    50ff., 105
Wholeness, 10, 60
Will, 51ff., 79
Winner, 83, 93
Wisconsin Schizophrenic Project, 39f.
Withdrawal, 26ff., 89, 109
Worship, 49, 61, 86

Index of Proper Names

Frankl, V., 94
Freud, S., 20, 31ff., 35, 140

Gendlin, E., 39
Gibb, J., 139
Gliedman, L., 37
Goffman, E., 102, 139
Gogarten, F., 107
Goodman, G., 5, 41, 142
Grotius, H., 127
Guerney, B., 30, 42

Hanson, P., 142
Harris, T., 47ff., 83, 86f., 93
Hegel, G., 90
Herberg, W., x, 153
Hillel, Rabbi, 69
Hiltner, S., 140
Hobbes, T., 90, 97
Hobbs, E., 144
Homans, G., 111, 151, 155
Howe, R., 138, 152
Hume, D., 97

Imber, S., 37
Isaacson, H., 37
James, M., 20, 47, 55ff., 93f.
Jesus Christ, 60ff., 73ff., 86, 94, 106, 128, 152
Job, 105
Jongeward, D., 20, 55ff., 93f.
Judah ben Ezekiel, Rabbi, 67
Justin Martyr, 68

Kant, I., 122
Katz, R., 138
Kelley, F., 37
Kelley, H., 102, 111, 125
Kierkegaard, S., 42, 94, 96, 102, 106f., 123f., 154f.
Kupfer, D., 67

Lake, F., 106
LaPiere, R., 148
Lapsley, J., 138

Leary, T., 37, 102, 111, 125
Leslie, R., 151
Levitt, B., 37
Lowen, A., 5
Luther, M., 42, 56, 57, 68, 95, 97, 102, 106

Machiavelli, N., 126f.
Marcel, G., 137
Maritain, J., 107, 108
Marney, C., 152
Maslow, A., 6
Masters, W., 32
May, R., 140
Mazur, R., 5
Michalson, C., 38
Miller, A., 131
Mink, O., 37
Morris, D., 122
Mowrer, H., 94–96

Nash, E., 37
Nathan, the prophet, 86, 105
Newman, J., 97, 143
Niebuhr, H.R., 106, 152
Niebuhr, R., 97, 120–129, 154f.

Oates, W., 137
O'Connell, W., 143
Oraison, M., 101, 106

Pannenberg, W., 139, 153
Pascal, B., 68
Paul, St., 23, 52ff., 71ff., 106
Penfield, W., 53
Pinter, H., 131
Plato, 133

Ramsey, P., 138, 155
Rogers, C., 17, 19, 38ff., 41
Roszak, T., 155

Satir, V., 138
Scheler, M., 138
Schmelke, Rabbi, 70
Schutz, W., 5, 102, 111, 155

Shostrom, E., 102
Snyder, R., 136, 151
Socrates, 94
Steiner, C., 48ff., 93, 102
Stone, A., 37
Suarez, F., 97
Sullivan, H., 102, 111
Szasz, T., 36

Tanner, I., 47
Teilhard de Chardin, 143
Tertullian, 58, 64, 70

Thibaut, J., 102, 111, 125
Tillich, P., 28, 140, 154
Toffler, A., 133
Truax, C., 37ff., 142f.

Vogel, J., 37

Walker, R., 37
Walsh, R., 37
Wesley, J., 67
Whitehorn, J., 39
Williams, T., 131

74 75 76 77 10 9 8 7 6 5 4 3 2 1